3/2. £2-45.

The Best of Thucydides

Fifteen extracts from
Thucydides' History of the Peloponnesian War
chosen and translated into English

THE
BEST OF
THUCYDIDES

Fifteen extracts from
Thucydides' History of the Peloponnesian War
chosen and translated into English

M G Dickson, CMG, MA

The Book Guild Ltd.
Sussex, England

To Godfrey Burchardt,
scholar and friend

The Book Guild Ltd.
25 High Street,
Lewes, Sussex

First published 1991
© M G Dickson 1991
Set in Baskerville
Typesetting by Ashford Setting & Design,
Ashford, Middlesex.
Printed in Great Britain by
Antony Rowe Ltd.,
Chippenham, Wiltshire.

British Library Cataloguing in Publication Data
Thucydides
    [History of the Peloponnesian War, selections] The best
    of Thucydides: fifteen extracts from Thucydides' History
    of the Peloponnesian War.
    1. Peloponnesian War
    I. [History of the Peloponnesian War, selections] II.
    Title III. Dickson, M.G. (Murray Graeme) 1911-
    938.05

ISBN 0 86332 547 5

CONTENTS

THE PELOPONNESIAN WAR

The Peloponnesian War (431-404 BC) was fought between Athens and her allies and dependencies on the one side, and Sparta (Lacedaemon) and her allies and dependencies on the other side. In the course of the conflict all the major cities of Greece on the mainland and most of the larger islands became involved. Hundreds of thousands of men were killed on land and sea during hostilities; many thousands of adult men were slaughtered when their city surrendered to the enemy. Large numbers of women and children were sold into slavery when their cities were captured or surrendered. In most cities there was a pro-Athenian party as well as a pro-Spartan party. Tension between the rival parties made civil strife an ever-present possibility. Civil strife (which the Greeks called *stasis*) was at its worst in Corcyra (the island now called Corfu). Thucydides' account of the conflict in this state is included here among the extracts from his history. Each side, when it was able to do so, devastated the crops of its enemy. Except in States able to import corn, there must have been a lowering of standards of nutrition. In many States, rural dwellers for the sake of their safety came to live within the city walls. In crowded, insanitary conditions disease was rife. In Athens itself there was a dreadful plague which is described in one of the excerpts. The war brought about a general lowering of standards of morality, public and private. The deterioration in public morality can be judged from the different treatment given to Mytilene in 429 when the male adult population was spared and the treatment given to Melos in 416 when every male adult was slaughtered and all the women and children sold into slavery.

In 404 BC Athens, exhausted by an unsuccessful attempt to conquer Sicily, surrendered. The long walls were demolished, to the sound of lutes, her navy was reduced to twelve ships and she and all her allies and dependencies became subject to Sparta.

Some forty years after her victory over Athens, Sparta lost the hegemony of Greece which passed to Thebes.

THUCYDIDES

Thucydides, son of Olorus, was an Athenian born sometime between 470 and 460 BC. His parents were well-to-do and it can be assumed that they gave him the best education available, which would have included oratory.

When war with Sparta broke out in 431 BC, Thucydides seems from the start to have foreseen that this was to be a major conflict and to have made up his mind to be its chronicler. In the second year of the war he suffered from the Plague but was among the few who survived the disease. He must have held official posts in which he proved his ability for in 424 BC he was given the rank of general and ordered to command a force to prevent the city of Amphipolis from falling into the hands of the Spartan general Brasidas. Thucydides arrived too late to protect the city but he successfully defended the neighbouring city of Eion which served as a port for Amphipolis. For his failure to save Amphipolis he was banished from Athens. Possessing gold mines in Thrace he was able to support himself during his exile. Where he spent the years of his exile is not known; it was probably in part of the Peloponnese under Spartan control. He died about the year 400 BC.

Thucydides took great care to discover by personal enquiry, and to record the course of the war and was meticulous about chronology. He divides each year into summer and winter and records what happened in each season. He is impartial in his judgements and free from prejudice. His own failure at Amphipolis is recorded in a completely objective manner. The only occasion when he allows his own imagination and beliefs to become apparent are the reports of speeches in public debates where, having discovered by enquiry the gist of what the speaker said he composes a speech such as the speaker is likely to have made. His personal views are also revealed in the occasional passages in which he comments on such matters as the decline in moral values evident in Athens after the Plague and the rise of politicians very inferior to Pericles.

Of his personal characteristics such as they emerge from his writings, M.I. Finley has written of him as 'a humourless man, pessimistic, highly intelligent, cold and reserved, at least on the surface but with strong inner tensions which occasionally break through the impersonal tone of his writing' (see the introduction to the translation in the Penguin classics).

In the scrupulous care he exercised in ascertaining what happened, his strict attention to chronology, his terse and concise narrative, his freedom from theological bias and personal prejudice, Thucydides produced a major historical work covering an important period in which he is virtually the sole authority.

EXCERPTS FROM THUCYDIDES HISTORY OF THE PELOPONNESIAN WAR

1

Thucydides' reasons for writing the History, and his treatment of the evidence

I, Thucydides the Athenian, wrote the history of the war between the Peloponnesians and the Athenians beginning at the very outbreak of the war, in the confident expectation that it was going to be a great conflict and more noteworthy than any which had preceded it. My belief was based on the fact that both sides were at the height of their power and preparedness. I saw too that the rest of the Greek world was likely to join one side or the other, some immediately, others after deliberating what course to take. This was certainly the greatest disturbance that had ever taken place in the Greek world, and it affected, too, part of the non-Greek world. You could almost say that all mankind was affected by it.

As regards the speeches I have recorded — some made just before the war began, others made during the course of the conflict — I have found it difficult to recall the exact words used in speeches which I listened to myself and those who informed me about speeches they had heard experienced the same difficulty. In such cases my method has been to keep as close as possible to the general gist of the views expressed and to make each speaker say what the situation seemed to require.

With regard to my reporting of the actual events of the war I have thought it right not to record the first account of the events which came to my notice or my own opinion of what probably took place. Either I was myself present at the incident described or I heard of it from an eye witness whose reliability I did my best to check. Even so the truth was not easy to discover. Different eye-witnesses give different accounts of the same event, either because they are partial to the one side or to the other, or because their memory is faulty.

It may be that to some my History will not make agreeable reading because of the absence in it of fanciful stories.

I shall be satisfied if what I have written is useful to those who wish to know what happened in the past and (human nature being what it is) may well happen again. I have not written to satisfy an immediate need among the public but to produce something which will last for ever.

2

Pericles' Funeral Oration

In the same winter, the Athenians, following their national custom gave a public funeral to those who had died in action during the war. The ceremony is conducted in this way:

Two days before the funeral ceremony a tent is erected in which the bones of the fallen are placed. Anyone can bring what offerings he likes for his own dead. At the funeral the bones are carried out in coffins made of cypress wood. There is one coffin for each tribe, in which the bones of that tribe are laid. There is also an empty decorated bier representing the remains of those who are missing; the bones in this bier have never been identified. Any one who wishes, be he citizen or foreigner, may accompany the procession of coffins. Women related to the dead, attend, to make their lamentations at the tomb. The coffins are brought to the public burial ground which is in the most beautiful area outside the city. Here they always bury those killed in war. The only exception is those who fell at Marathon who were buried on the site of the battle because it was felt that their valour and achievement were quite exceptional.

After the burial a man chosen by the city for his outstanding intellectual gifts and judgement makes a speech in praise of the dead. On this first such occasion of the war the man chosen to speak was Pericles, son of Xanthippus. At the appropriate moment he stepped forward from the burial ground and, mounting a dais which had been erected, spoke as follows:

'Many of those who in the past have spoken on these occasions have praised the institution of a funeral oration. I do not share their view. The men whom we are honouring showed their worth by their actions and it seems to me sufficient if we honour them

15

by our actions as we are doing now by giving them a State Funeral. We should not let the honour due to them depend on the merits of what one speaker says. For it is difficult to speak on these occasions in due measure, neither exaggerating nor depreciating the merits and achievements of the fallen soldiers. It is easy to give offence by saying too much or too little in their praise. However the fact is that the giving of a funeral oration is a custom initiated by our forefathers and it is my duty to do my best to meet the wishes and expectations of each one of you.

'I shall begin by speaking about our ancestors for it is right and proper to honour them by recalling what they did. This land of ours has always been occupied by the same people who because of their courage and virtue have handed it down from generation to generation as a free country.

'Still more should we honour our fathers. For to the land they inherited they added the empire which we rule and they have organized the state so that it is able to look after itself in peace and in war. Of the warlike deeds by which our Fathers defended the state against its enemies Greek and foreign I do not wish to speak at length. What I wish to speak to you about is the kind of spirit in which we have always faced our trials and the character of our constitution. After that, I will speak in praise of the fallen. I think this sort of approach is most suitable and will meet with the approval of all those present, citizens and foreigners.

'Our constitution does not copy those of our neighbours. On the contrary, it serves rather as an example to others who imitate us: it is called a democracy because power resides in the many not the few. In civil disputes between individuals all are equal before the law. When it comes to choosing someone for a position of authority the choice is made not from consideration of rank or family but solely on the merit and ability of the man being considered. If any one is capable of rendering good service to the State neither poverty nor want of illustrious family or rank will stand in his way.

'We conduct public affairs in a spirit of freedom and openness and we show the same spirit in our day-to-day relations with each other. We do not quarrel with our neighbour about the way he chooses to enjoy himself nor do we give him those disapproving looks which, though they do no real harm, may give offence.

16

'In the conduct of political affairs we keep to the laws. This is because we have deep respect for the law. We give obedience to those in authority and we obey the laws, especially those which exist for the relief of the oppressed and those unwritten laws which we agree it is shameful to break.

'Another important aspect of our way of living is that when we can enjoy a break from work there are many kinds of recreation open to us including contests and sacrifices which go on throughout the year. In our homes we find beauty and good taste which in our daily lives drive away care.

'The greatness of our city attracts to it all manner of good things from every quarter of the world so it seems to us natural to enjoy the products of other lands just as we enjoy home grown produce.

'Our provision of military security differs widely from that of our enemies. Our city is open to anyone in the world to visit and observe. We do not carry out periodic expulsions of non-citizens in order to prevent any foreigner from discovering secrets of our defence. For we rely not so much on secret weapons and stratagems as on our courage in action. In the training of the young our enemy relies on arduous exercises to develop courage. We, on the contrary live our lives free from these restraints but we are equal to them when it comes to facing dangers. Here is proof of this. When the Spartans invade our land they do not come alone but accompanied by all their allies while we when we campaign abroad fight alone and on most occasions are successful. The enemy's army has never encountered our full resources in manpower for some of our fighting men are employed in naval service and some of our land forces may be engaged in operations elsewhere in Greece. When the enemy engages a detachment of our land forces and gains the upper hand they boast that they have overcome our whole land force and if they are worsted they say they have been defeated by our full army.

'There are a few matters about our way of life which I think deserve mention:

'We do not allow our love of beauty to lead us into extravagance nor do we allow our fondness for philosophical thought and discussion to make us soft.

'We regard wealth as a possession which provides an opportunity for action, not as something to boast about. No one

17

need be ashamed of being poor. What is shameful is to make no effort to escape from poverty.

'Each one of us in interested not only in his own affairs but in the affairs of the State. Even those who are very fully occupied with their own affairs are often extremely well informed about State political matters. It is a peculiarity of ours that if a man concerns himself solely with his own affairs and takes no part in the city's political life, we do not regard him as a sensible quiet person who minds his own business. We regard him as not doing his duty towards the State.

'We Athenians make up our own minds about the right policy for the state to follow, or we put forward our views for proper discussion. We do not see any conflict here between words and deeds. It is right to discuss issues before rushing into action. It is right to have a full discussion in advance before decisions are made about action to be taken. What is wrong is to undertake risks without having first weighed all the possible consequences of our action.

'Another matter where we differ from other peoples is that they are often brave and daring because they have not considered what they are rushing into. When they see what they have let themselves into they are afraid. We on the contrary regard those as really brave who are aware of the dangers of their action but resolve to act in spite of the risks.

'Another characteristic of us Athenians is that we make friends with those on whom we have conferred kindnesses not with those who have shown kindness to us. This makes our friendships more lasting because we want to keep alive the friendship by bestowing further kindnesses.

'Taking into consideration all these aspects of our way of life I declare that Athens is an education to Greece. And I also state my belief that each one of our citizens in all the manifold aspects of his existence can feel that he is in control of his life and can conduct himself with all the grace and versatility of which he is capable.

'It is not necessary to express in words of praise the glory of our city which I have tried to describe for the truth of what I have said can be seen in the power which Athens possesses. We do not need a Homer or anyone else to sing the praises of our state in language which will please for the moment but fall short of the truth. Our adventurous and enterprising spirit has sent our people into every sea and land and wherever we have been we have left memorials of the good we have done to our friends and the damage we have inflicted on our enemies.

'This is the city from which the men we are honouring today could not bear to be parted. For her they nobly lived and nobly died. It is only right that we who are left should be willing to undergo hardship in her service.

'I have spoken at length about our city and our way of life because I wanted to make it clear that in this way there's more at stake for us than there is for the other combatants. I wanted to set my words and praise for the fallen in the context of what they were fighting for.

'Now I have described the most important characteristics of our city and our way of life to which the courage of these men and others have added glory and honour. You would not find many cities in Greece where it could be said that such words of praise as I have used are matched by the achievements of the city.

'The end that has befallen these men whom we are mourning seems to me to prove their courage and its final consummation. Some of them no doubt had their faults but they blotted out their faults by their gallantry in defence of the city and did more good in this way than any harm they did in their private lives. None of them was weakened by the desire to preserve his wealth or by the hope that he might escape from poverty and grow rich. It seemed to them that more important than these objectives was the need to curb the enemy's pride and offer resistance to his attacks, considering this to be the more honourable course of action. As for success or failure they left that in the hands of Hope and when they were in battle they put their trust in themselves. They chose to stand firm and risk death rather than give in and save themselves. They fled from the reproaches of men and stood their ground and in a brief moment of time — the climax of their lives — at the height of their glory, and without any fear they were taken away from us.

'Such were these men, who proved themselves worthy of their city. We who are left may hope to be spared that fate but we must resolve to keep alive the same daring spirit which they showed against the enemy. It is not just a matter of appreciating the strategic advantage of resisting the enemy's attacks. I could talk at length about the advantages of beating back the enemy's advances into our territory. You are already familiar with the arguments in favour of this course of action.

'Instead I would rather ask you every day of your life to look with wonder at the might of Athens and to become a lover of our city. When you ponder on her greatness recollect that what made her great was the spirit of enterprising and daring men who knew what it was their duty to do and who were ashamed to fall below the standard expected of them. They were resolved that if they failed to fulfil their aim no one should say it was because they lacked courage. They gave the greatest contribution that it was in their power to give — they gave their lives for the sake of every one of us. For themselves they won a reward which will last for ever. They won the most splendid of sepulchres — not the tomb where they now lie, but the glory of a name which will be an inspiration to those who come after them. For the whole earth is the sepulchre of famous men. Their memorial is not the inscription engraved on their tombs in their native land. It is not this that marks them out. No, in foreign lands also their memory will survive not in any visible form but in men's hearts. Make up your minds to be like them. Know well that there is no happiness without freedom and to remain free you must be courageous. There must be eternal vigilance in face of the dangers of war. Any man of spirit would find it more painful to meet death like a weakling than to perish in battle in a death which cannot be foreseen while he is in the fulness of his strength and in the confidence that he is doing his patriotic duty.

'To those of you who are parents of the dead I should like to offer not commiseration but encouragement and condolence. We live in a world which is full of changes and chances. But it is good fortune for a man to end his life in an honourable way and it is your good fortune to be able to lament their passing with honour.

'The lives of the men whom we are now honouring were so ordered that for them death and blessedness came together. I know it is difficult for you who have been bereaved to believe this. When you see other people enjoying their good fortune you will be reminded of what you have lost. Sorrow comes not when we are deprived of blessings we have never enjoyed but when we lose something which we have been accustomed to enjoy. Those of you who are of an age when you can have children must bear up bravely and hope you will have other children. These children will console you a little for those whom you have lost. They will benefit the city by keeping up the population and ensuring that we have sound policies on defence. For it is impossible for anyone to put forward fair and honest proposals about war and peace if he does not have any children whose lives are put at stake by the decisions reached.'

'To those of you who have passed the age when you can have children I would say this. For most of your life you have enjoyed the good fortune of having children and for the part that remains you must find consolation in the fame of those who perished. Our sense of honour is one of those things which does not disappear in old age. In the infirmity of old age it is not making profits that brings delight but being respected by other people.

'For those of you who are sons or brothers of the fallen I foresee a hard struggle ahead of you. For everyone speaks highly of the dead. It will be hard for you to exceed their valour and it will be difficult for you to be regarded as equalling them in courage, or coming near to their standard.

'Perhaps I should say something about those of you who are the widows or the mothers of those who have fallen. I think I can say to you all that needs to be said quite briefly. Be true to the qualities which Nature has given to women. The greatest glory of a woman is to be least talked about by men whether in praise or in criticism.

'And now I have said what I had to say as the law requires. Our offerings to the dead have been made. Their children will be supported by the State until they come of age. This is the crown and prize which Athens offers to the dead and those they leave behind in recognition of the ordeal they have undergone. Where the rewards for valour are the greatest there you will find the best of our citizens. And now when you have paid your tribute to your dear ones, you should each go home.'

3

Pericles on Athenian Imperialism

It is right and proper for you to support the imperial power of Athens. You all take pride in it. You cannot enjoy the glory it brings and at the same time avoid the burdens it lays on you. Don't make the mistake of thinking that the one issue on which we are fighting is servitude or freedom. You are fighting to prevent the loss of our empire and the dangers arising from the hatred we have incurred in the exercise of our dominion. It is not possible for us now to withdraw from our imperial position, if any of you in the present crisis are attracted by the honesty of such an unambitious course of action, for, to speak frankly, what you hold is a tyranny. It may have been wrong to take it but to let it go would be highly dangerous. If those who wish to give up our empire were able to convert others to their point of view the State would quickly be ruined. The result would be the same as if they could live independently on their own. For those who seek only to live a quiet life are only able to do so if they have the support of those who are more active than they are themselves. People who desire only to live a quiet life are useless to an imperial city, though they may help a dependent state to endure its subordinate status in safety.

4

Pericles' control over the Assembly, and the character of his successors

Pericles outlived the beginning of the war by two years and six months. After his death the correctness of his foresight about the war became more evident.

Pericles by his rank, intelligence and known integrity was able to exercise an independent control over the people — to lead them rather than be led by them. As he never sought power by improper means he was never compelled to flatter the people. On the contrary he enjoyed so high a reputation that he could afford to anger them by speaking against their current mood. If he saw that their spirits were unreasonably elated he would with a few words reduce them to a state of alarm. But if he saw them struck with panic he could immediately restore their confidence. In short, what was nominally a democracy became in his hands government by the first citizen.

With those who came after him it was different. Being more on a level with each other and each striving for supremacy they ended by entrusting the affairs of the State to the whims of the populace. This, as might have been expected in a great and sovereign state, led to a host of blunders and amongst them the Sicilian expedition.

Yet after losing most of their fleet and other forces in Sicily and with civil strife already disturbing Athens they could still for three years hold out against their original adversaries joined not only by Sicilians but also by their own allies who were mainly in revolt and at last by the Persian King's son, Cyrus, who provided funds for the Peloponnesian navy. Nor did they finally succumb until they fell victims of their own internal strife. So abundant were the resources from which the genius of Pericles had foreseen an easy victory over the Peloponnesians alone.

5

The Plague in Athens

In the second year of the war the Plague broke out in Athens. There had been previous attacks of this disease in the neighbourhood of Lemnos and in some other places but there was no record of any previous outbreak as virulent and deadly as that which afflicted Athens. At first doctors did not know how to treat the disease and many of them fell victims to it, perhaps because they were in close contact with the disease. No human skill or knowledge was of any use in treating the disease. Prayers offered in temples, consultation of oracles and such like all proved to be of no avail. In the end, overcome by the disaster, people ceased to make such appeals.

The Plague originated, it was believed, in Ethiopia or Upper Egypt, and then spread to Egypt, Libya and the domain of the Persian Emperor. In Athens the disease struck suddenly. It first appeared in the district of Piraeus. People said that the Peloponnesians must have poisoned the reservoirs; at that time there were no wells in Piraeus. From there the disease spread to the upper city. By now deaths were very numerous.

I shall leave it to other writers, whether doctors or laymen, to describe the medical aspects of the Plague, its causes and the reason why the attack in Athens was so deadly. I shall confine myself to describing what it was like so that if there is another outbreak those who have read what I have written will recognize the disease for what it is. I myself suffered from the Plague and observed others suffering from it.

That year it was generally agreed had been exceptionally free from diseases and minor illnesses. But those who had suffered other illnesses caught the plague eventually. People in normal good health suddenly began to experience a burning sensation in the head. Their eyes became red and inflamed. Inside the mouth there was bleeding from the throat and tongue. Breathing became unnatural and the breath had a bad odour. This was followed by sneezing and a sore throat. Soon afterwards the disease descended to the chest where it caused much pain and coughing. The next part of the body to be affected was the stomach which became very upset. Every kind of bile to which the medical profession has given a name was vomited up. All this caused much pain and distress to the sufferer. There was ineffectual retching causing violent spasms. These symptoms abated but sometimes only after a long period of distress. Externally the body was not very hot to the touch, nor did it become pale. In some patients the skin became red and livid and small pustules and ulcers appeared. There was a feeling of intense burning so that victims could not bear to be covered by even the lightest clothing or very fine linen, but chose to lie naked. They felt a strong urge to plunge into cold water. Many of those who had no one to look after them did actually immerse themselves in the water tanks in an effort to quench a thirst that was in fact unquenchable whether they drank much or a little. All the time they suffered from insomnia and the inability to rest quietly.

In the period when the disease was at its height, so far from wasting the body showed surprising powers of endurance. By the ninth or eighth day of the fever when many died, the body still had some strength. For those who survived this critical period the disease then affected the stomach and the bowels, causing ulceration and uncontrollable diarrhoea. Many died later from the weakness this caused.

The disease worked itself downwards through the whole body, beginning in the head and even when people escaped the worst results it left the mark of its attack on the extremities, the genitals, the fingers and the toes and some who survived the plague lost the use of these parts of the body. Some became blind, some when they began to recover lost their memory. They did not know who they were and could not recognize their friends.

There was one phenomenon which marked this disease as different from others. Birds and beasts which feed on human flesh would not touch the bodies of victims of the plague which lay unburied. Those that did eat the flesh of victims died.

Evidence of this may be found in the complete disappearance of birds of prey. For its effect on animals, dogs, being domesticated creatures, provided the best means of observing how they were affected by the disease.

This was the general nature of the disease but I have omitted mentioning some peculiar symptoms which affected individual victims. None of the usual illnesses which people got affected people at that time but for those who did suffer from other illnesses, the illness usually ended in the Plague.

Some died in neglect, others died in spite of every kind of care and attention. As for a recognized method of treatment for sufferers there was none. A treatment which might benefit one sufferer could make another worse. Those with strong constitutions were no more able to resist the disease than those with weak constitutions.

The Plague killed all alike including those who were well cared for and given good food.

The most terrible thing of all was the hopelessness and apathy of those who became aware that they had caught the disease. They immediately abandoned all hope of recovery, and this weakened their powers of resistance.

It was terrible too to see people who had caught the disease by nursing the sick, dying like sheep. Some regarded it as a point of honour to help the afflicted. Such people felt ashamed to have regard to their own safety and went to the help of their friends even though they were so overwhelmed by the calamity that they neglected the customary rules of lamenting the dead.

Those who took the most care for the sick and dying were those who had themselves survived an attack. They knew what it was like and were in confident spirits for the disease did not strike the same person twice or if it did, it did not kill him. Such people were congratulated by others. In their elation at their recovery they believed that they could not be killed by any other disease.

A factor which made things worse than they would otherwise have been was the influx into the city of country dwellers. These people were specially liable to catch the disease for having no houses they lived in badly ventilated huts. In the hot season they died in great numbers. The corpses of the dead lay piled on top of each other and in the streets, seriously afflicted people staggered about trying to get at the fountains in order to quench their raging thirst. The temples where many people took shelter were full of the dead and dying. For the calamity was so overpowering that people neglected every rule of the temples and of religion. All the funeral customs that used to be observed were ignored. People buried their dead as fast as they could. Some adopted shameless methods of disposing of their dead. Lacking any resources because so many of their family had already died they would arrive at a pyre prepared by someone else, lay their own corpse on it and set the pyre alight, or finding a pyre already burning would dump their corpse on top and quickly disappear.

The Plague affected Athens in many ways. It resulted in an unprecedented outbreak of lawlessness. Seeing swift and sudden changes of fortune when rich men died and those who previously had possessed nothing now inherited wealth people ventured openly on acts of self-indulgence which previously they would have tried to conceal. Many people resolved to spend what money they had very quickly and to spend it on pleasure since money and life seemed equally ephemeral. As for honest and honourable conduct no one thought much about it since everyone considered that before he could gain a good reputation for such conduct he might be dead. It was generally agreed that the right thing to aim at was the pleasure of the moment, and anything that made it possible. Neither fear of the gods nor respect for human laws exercised any restraining influence on people — for people saw that those who respected divine and human laws fared no better than those who disregarded them. As for criminal offences, no one expected to live long enough to be brought to trial and punished.

This was the calamity which befell Athens. Times were indeed hard with people dying in the city and the land outside being ravaged by the enemy.

6

The Siege of Plataea and the End of Plataea

Plataea was a small city which had for a long time been an ally of Athens. During the Persian invasion at the time of the Emperor Darius, Plataea was the only city which sent a contingent to help the Athenians drive back the invaders at Marathon. In the later invasion, at the time of the Emperor Xerxes, after the defeat of the Persian fleet at Salamis, the Persian land forces assembled near Plataea and were defeated by a Greek army under the Spartan commander Pausanias. The Plataeans took a full part in defeating the invader.

Their very creditable record in the past was of no avail to the Plataeans in the Peloponnesian War. As allies of Athens they were bound, sooner or later, to come under attack by the Peloponnesians.

The account by Thucydides of the Siege of Plataea gives a good picture of contemporary methods of siege warfare. Most readers will regret the tragic end of the episode.

* * *

Thucydides writes:

The next summer the Peloponnesians and their allies instead of invading Attica marched against Plataea. They were under the command of the Spartan King Archidamus son of Zeuxidamus. He encamped opposite Plataea and was about to begin laying waste the land when the Plataeans sent a deputation which addressed him as follows:

'Archidamus and Spartans, in attacking our land you are

29

acting in a dishonourable way unworthy of yourselves and your ancestors. Remember what the Spartan Pausanias, son of Cleombrotus said and did when he freed Greece from the Persians with the aid of those Greeks who willingly shared the dangers of a battle near our city. Pausanias sacrificed in the market-place of Plataea to Zeus the Liberator and calling to witness all the allies handed over to the Plataeans their city and land to hold them free and independent guaranteed for ever against unprovoked attack and foreign domination. This was the promise given by your ancestors because of the courage and zeal which we showed at that time of danger.

But now you are acting contrary to those promises. In conjunction with our enemies, the Thebans, you are bent on subjugating our land.

We appeal to you in the name of the gods who witnessed those oaths and in the name of the gods of our country and the gods of your country not to break those oaths by making an unprovoked attack on us but allow us to continue to be independent.'

At this point Archidamus interrupted the envoys and said 'What you say, O Plataeans, would be fair enough if you yourselves matched your deeds and words. You swore that you would hold your city in independence but you have not done so. You have put your city into subjection to Athens. It is to free you from dependence on Athens that this army you see here was assembled and this war undertaken. You should remember this, and yourselves be true to the oaths you took. If you cannot do this then do what we have already asked you to do, preserve your independence and join neither side in war. Be friendly to both sides and be at war with neither. This will satisfy us.' Thus spake Archidamus.

The Plataean envoys returned to their city and reported what had been said.

The Plataeans replied that they were not able to do as the Spartans wished, without the consent of Athens. For their wives and children were in Athens. When the Peloponnesian army withdrew the Athenians might come and take over their city, or the Thebans who have the right under the proposed Terms of the Treaty, might attempt to seize control.

Archidamus then urged the Plataeans to consider another proposal to this effect:

30

'Hand over the city with all its houses to us Lacedaemonians, show us the boundaries of your land and the numbers of your fruit trees and all your other possessions that can be quantified. You yourselves go away to any place that you wish for as long as the war lasts. When the war is over we will hand back to you what you have handed over. Until then we will hold everything in trust for you, sending to you sufficient produce for your needs.'

The Plataean envoys returned once more to the city and discussed this latest proposal in the Assembly. It was decided that they must first inform the Athenians of this proposal and if Athens agreed to it, they would accept this offer. They asked King Archidamus in the meantime to grant an armistice and not lay waste their land. Archidamus agreed to grant an armistice for so long as it took for envoys to travel to Athens and return. During this time the Peloponnesians did not lay waste the lands of the Plataeans.

The reply from the Athenians was:

'Men of Plataea, during all the time when we have been allies we have never done you wrong. Now we will not neglect you but will come to your assistance with all the force we can muster. We invoke you by the oaths you swore not to depart from our alliance.'

The Plataeans having heard this message decided not to break the alliance but if necessary, to endure seeing their land laid waste and whatever other hardships they had to face. The envoys did not go out again. Instead, heralds announced from the walls that it was impossible for the Plataeans to do what the Lacedaemonians called upon them to do.

Archidamus then called upon the gods and heroes of Plataea to witness and declared 'Gods and heroes of the land of Plataea I call upon you to witness that from the first it was not in an aggressive spirit but because those people had broken their agreements that we invaded their land in which our fathers offered their prayers to you before they fought and defeated the Persians and which you made a place of good omen for battle by Hellenes. We shall not be acting aggressively now. We have made a number of reasonable proposals but they have not been accepted. Give us your aid and see that punishment falls on those who were first to do wrong and that we may succeed in our aim which is justified revenge.'

31

After this appeal to the gods Archidamus set his army into action against the Plataeans.

Using trees they had cut down, the army built a stockade round the city to prevent sorties.

Then they built a mound against the city. They were confident that they would soon take the city because of the large number of men in the Peloponnesian army.

They cut down timber from Mount Cithaeron and used it to build a framework laying the baulks of timber so that they crossed each other at right angles and fixed it on either side of the mound so as to keep the materials inside the mound in position and not allow it to spread all over the place. They made the mound from wood and stones and earth and anything else that would fill up the space.

This work went on continuously for seventy days and nights. While some men slept or ate their meals others took their place at the work. In each contingent Spartan officers kept the men at their work.

When the Plataeans saw the mound going up, higher and higher, they built a wooden wall and placed it on top of the city wall opposite the place where the mound was going up. They filled this wooden wall with bricks taken from nearby houses. The wood acted as a bond giving the whole wall stability as its height increased. They fitted on top of the wall a covering of skins and hides to preserve the woodwork from catching fire from fire-arrows and to protect the men working there. This wall rose to a great height and opposite it the mound too rose higher and higher.

The Plataeans then adopted another plan. They demolished the part of their city wall which was opposite the mound and removed the earth from inside the mound, carrying it inside the city.

To counteract this stratagem the Peloponnesians made reed mats which they packed tightly with clay. This more solid material was more difficult for the Plataeans to remove than loose earth.

Foiled in this stratagem the Plataeans abandoned it. Instead they dug a tunnel from inside the city to the base of the mound. They carried away the earth at the base of the mound and took it inside the city.

For some time the besiegers did not understand why the

32

mound did not rise in height as they put more and more earth on top of it. Then at last they realised that earth was moved from the base of the mound and while more earth was put on top of the mound, earth inside the mound was settling down to fill the gap where the Plataeans removed earth from the base and carried it away through the tunnel.

In spite of this success the Plataeans began to fear that because of their small numbers they could not hold out indefinitely against the large numbers of the enemy. So they adopted another defensive measure. They abandoned work on the structure opposite the mound and starting from each end of it built a crescent-shaped wall bending inwards into the city. So if the main wall was captured they would still have the protection of the crescent-shaped wall and the enemy would have the slow work of constructing another mound.

The Peloponnesians had now failed to achieve any success by their mound and their siege engines, and were faced by the structure erected by the Plataeans opposite the mound. They concluded that it would not be possible to capture the city by the usual methods of siege warfare and they would have to prepare to blockade the city by building a wall of circumvallation which would surround the city. In fact they considered every possible way of taking the city without having to undergo the expense of a long siege.

But they thought they would first try to burn down the city which was not a large one and if a favourable wind sprang up the fire might destroy the city. So they threw bundles of wood from the top of the mound into the space between the mound and the city wall. With so many taking part in the work this space was soon filled. They then threw bundles of firewood as far as they could into the middle of the city. They added sulphur and pitch to the wood and then set fire to it.

The resulting conflagration was greater than any that had ever been seen before, at least as regards fires caused by human agency though it did not exceed fires caused in mountain forests when the wind causes branches to rub together and start a fire. The fire caused by the Spartans very nearly destroyed the city of the Plataeans who had escaped so many previous dangers. A large part of the city was rendered uninhabitable and if a wind had sprung up the Plataeans would not have escaped destruction. However this did not occur. Now it is said that there happened to occur a heavy outpour of rain, accompanied by thunder which put out the fire and saved the city.

After this failure the Peloponnesians dismissed the greater part of their army but retained a certain number of men to build a wall of circumvallation. They divided the work among the various cities who contributed contingents to the army. They dug a ditch on either side of the wall and from there extracted material to make bricks. The work was completed about the time of the rising of Arcturus.

The Peloponnesians then left sufficient men to garrison half the wall (as for the other half of the wall the Boeotians provided men to guard it). The rest of their army they dismissed.

The Plataeans had already sent their women and children to Athens together with the old men and others not fit for combatant duty. Those who remained to withstand the siege numbered 400 men together with eighty Athenians and 110 women to do the cooking. There were no others, citizens or slaves, in the city.

Thus began the Siege of Plataea.

In the winter of the third year of the siege, the Plataeans were distressed by the shortage of food and having lost hope of any help coming from Athens or any other means of relief, formed a plan of escape in conjunction with those Athenians who were with them in the besieged city. At first the plan was that all inside the city should leave it and escape over the walls erected by the enemy. The plan had been suggested by Theaenetis son of Tolmides, a soothsayer and Eupompides son of Daimachus, a general. Later, half the men withdrew from the plan considering it too dangerous. There remained two hundred and twenty men willing to attempt this way of escape, which was carried out in the following manner. Ladders were made to equal the height of the enemy's wall which they measured by the layers of bricks on the side facing them which had not been thoroughly whitewashed. These were counted by many persons at once and though some got the number wrong most got the correct number, particularly as they counted over and over again and the wall was not far away and could be seen clearly enough for their purpose. The length required for the ladders was then obtained being calculated from the breadth of the brick.

Now the wall of the Peloponnesians was constructed as follows. There were two circuits, one facing the city to prevent the exodus of the besieged men and an outer wall to prevent an Athenian force attempting to relieve the city, the two walls being about sixteen feet apart. The space between the two walls was occupied by quarters for the guards and built in one block giving the appearance of a single thick wall with battlements on either side.

At intervals of every ten battlements there were towers of considerable height and of the same breadth as the wall reaching right across from the outer to the inner wall with no means of passing except through the middle. Accordingly on stormy and wet nights the battlements were deserted, guard being kept from the towers, which were not far apart and were roofed in above.

Such was the structure of the wall by which the Plataeans were blockaded. The Plataeans, when their preparations were completed, waited for a stormy night of wind and rain, with no moon. They were led by those who had planned the escape. First they crossed the ditch which ran round the town and then made for the enemy's main wall, unobserved by those on guard who could not see them in the dark or hear them because of the noise made by the wind. Besides, the escapers kept a good distance apart from each other so that they could not be betrayed by the clash of their arms. They were also lightly equipped and were shod only on one foot to prevent them slipping in the mud. They came up to the battlements at one of the intermediate places which they knew to be unguarded. Those who carried the ladders went first and placed them in position. Next twelve light armed men equipped with only a dagger and a breastplate mounted, led by Ammias son of Corvelus who was the first on the wall. His followers mounted after him, going six to each tower. After these came another party of light troops armed with spears whose shields were carried by men behind who were to hand them over when they found themselves in the presence of the enemy.

After a good number had climbed on to the wall they were discovered by one of the guards when a Plataean laying hold of the battlements knocked down a tile which fell and broke with a loud noise. The alarm was sounded and the Peloponnesian soldiers rushed to the wall, but because of the darkness and wind could not see where the trouble was. Most of them remained at their posts not knowing where they were needed to assist. The Plataeans inside the town chose that moment to make a sortie against the wall of the Peloponnesians on the side opposite to that where the escape was being made. Meanwhile the three hundred Peloponnesians held in reserve for use in emergencies went outside the wall in the direction of the alarm. Fire signals of an attack were also sent up towards Thebes. But the Plataeans in the town at once displayed a number of others prepared beforehand to make the enemy's signals unintelligible and to prevent the enemy's friends from getting a clear idea of what was happening before their comrades who had gone out should have made a successful escape.

Meanwhile the first of the scaling parties that had got up, captured both the towers and put to death the guards. They then took up positions inside the towers to prevent anyone coming through against them. They set up ladders from the wall and sent up several men on to the towers. Then from the summit and base of the towers they used their missiles to drive away any that came up while their main body planted a number of ladders against the wall and, knocking down the battlements, passed over between the towers. Each man as soon as he got over took up his position at the edge of the ditch hurling arrows and darts at any enemy who came along the wall to stop the passage of his comrades. When all had crossed over the party on the towers came down, the last of them not without difficulty and proceeded to the ditch just as the three hundred came up carrying torches. The Plataeans, standing on the edge of the ditch in the dark could see the enemy clearly and discharged their arrows and darts upon the unprotected part of the enemy's bodies, while they themselves could not be clearly seen in the darkness because of the torches. Thus even the last of them got over the ditch though not without effort and difficulty. For ice had formed in the ditch, not strong enough to walk on but of that watery kind which often comes when the wind is more from the east than the north and the snow which this wind had brought during the night had made the level of the water in the ditch rise so that they could scarcely breast it as they crossed. Still it was mainly the violence of the storm that enabled them to escape at all.

Setting off from the ditch the Plataeans went, all together, along the road leading to Thebes keeping the chapel of the hero Androcrates upon their right. For they considered that the last road which the Peloponnesians would expect them to take would be that leading to their enemy's country. Indeed they could see the enemy in pursuit with torches along the Athens road towards Cithaeron and Droscephalae. After going for rather more than a mile along the road to Thebes the Plataeans turned off and took the road leading to the mountains and so made good their escape to Athens. Two hundred and twelve men in all reached Athens, some of the men having turned back into the town before getting over the wall and one archer having been taken prisoner at the outer ditch. Meanwhile the Peloponnesians gave up the pursuit and returned to their posts. The Plataeans left in the town, knowing nothing of what had happened and informed by those that had turned back that not a man had escaped, sent out a herald as soon as it was day to ask for a truce for the recovery of the dead bodies, and then learning the truth abandoned the idea.

In the fourth year of the siege the Plataeans whose provisions were now exhausted could no longer continue to endure a siege. They surrendered their city of the Lacedaemonians.
This is how it came about.

The Peloponessian commander had ordered a general assault on the city's wall. Observing the assault he recognized that the besieged were now too weak to defend the wall. He could easily have taken the city by storm but he did not wish to do that. He had been told by army HQ in Sparta that he must not capture the city by force. The Spartans thought that when the war between Athens and Sparta ended the peace treaty might require each side to hand back all cities they had taken by force: if Plataea could be induced to surrender voluntarily Sparta would not be required to hand it over.

So the Peloponnesian commander sent a herald to the Plataeans who told them:

'If you will of your own accord surrender the city to the Lacedaemonians and submit yourselves to their decisions, they will punish only the guilty and do everything according to justice.'

The Plataeans, who were now in the last stages of exhaustion handed over their city. The Peloponnesians fed them for some days until the judges, five in number, arrived from Sparta.

When the judges arrived they made no accusation against the Plataeans but each man was brought forward and asked one

37

question: 'Had he done anything to help the Lacedaemonians during the present war?'

This method of procedure provoked the Plataeans to ask permission to speak at greater length and appointed as their spokesmen, Astymachus son of Asuphalaus, and Lacon son of Aemnestus who represented Spartan interests in Plataea. These men spoke as follows:

'When we surrendered our city to you, O Lacedaemonians, we did not expect to have to undergo a trial of this nature, but one of the more usual nature. When we consented to be tried by you we expected to receive fair treatment. But now we have been disappointed on both counts. For we have good reason to suspect that the issue involved is of the gravest nature, a matter of life or death to us and we fear you will not be impartial judges. We draw these conclusions from the fact that no charge has been made against us. We have had to ask leave to speak and the brief question we are each required to answer is a very unfair one. If we answer truthfully we will appear to condemn ourselves, but if we answer falsely our untruthfulness will be readily proved. Surrounded by difficulties on every side we are forced to take what seems to be a safer course and say something on our behalf. For to men in our position not to do so might cause us eventually to reproach ourselves with this thought that had we said the right word it might have saved us.

'Another difficulty facing us is the difficulty of persuading you to see our point of view. If we were strangers to each other it might be to our advantage to give evidence of matters which were not familiar to you but whatever we say is likely to be well known to you and we fear that you have already decided that anything that we can say in our favour is outweighed by what you regard as matters to our disadvantage.

'In the war against the Persians and in the peace that followed it we proved ourselves to be good and true men and we have not now been the first to break the peace. We were the only Boeotians who rallied to the cause of the freedom of Greece. Though we are not a maritime people we took part in the sea-battle at Artemisium and in the battle that was fought here on our land we stood side by side with Pausanias and yourselves and in the dangers that at that time threatened the Greeks we played our part beyond our resources.

'And in particular O Lacedaemonians, at a time when you

38

were in deadly danger after the earthquake and the revolt of the Helots and their occupation of Ithome we sent a third part of our citizen force to succour you. That is something you ought not to forget.

'In the great actions of the past we were proud to play our part. It was only later that we became your enemies. You were responsible for that. For when the Thebans oppressed us and we sought an alliance with you, you rejected our request and bade us seek an alliance with Athens, for they were near and you were far away. In the course of the present war you have never suffered — nor were you likely to suffer, any significant injury from us. If we did not revolt from Athenian rule there was nothing wrong in that, for they helped us against the Thebans when you held back. It would have been dishonourable for us to desert them, when they had helped us and we were under an obligation to them.

'As for the Thebans they have done us many wrongs in the past and you are aware of their latest wrong-doing which has brought us to our present plight. They attempted to sieze our city during a period of peace and on a day of festival. In accordance with the sanction of universal law, we were justified in resisting their unprovoked assault and we cannot reasonably be asked to suffer on that account. If you will decide what you ought to do now simply by considering what it is to your advantage to do you will show yourselves to be not true judges of what it is honourable to do but to determine the issues simply by considering what is to your advantage.

'The Thebans may seem serviceable to you now but remember that we and the other Greeks were far more serviceable to you at that time when you stood in greater danger. For now you are attacking others and are a threat to them. But at the time of the Persian invasion when they were seeking to enslave us all, these Thebans were on the side of the Persians. It is only fair that you should set against our present errors — if indeed we have erred — the zeal we showed against the Persians, and if you do, you will find that the zeal far outweighs our present offence and also it was shown at a time when it was rare for any Greek state to show its courage by withstanding the might of Persia. At that time the greater praise went to those who, instead of intriguing for their own safety were ready to risk taking the most honourable course, dangerous though it was.

'And now we fear we are to be destroyed because we chose the Athenians for the sake of doing the right thing, rather than you for the sake of seeking our advantage. You should consider that your true advantage lies only in this, to show an everlasting gratitude to those who were the best of your allies for their valour whilst also securing what may be to your advantage in the present situation . . . .

'Look at the sepulchres of your fathers who were slain by the Persians and buried in our land whom we have honoured year after year by giving to them public offerings of garments and other gifts as custom requires; also we bring them the first fruits of the earth — gifts by friendly people from a friendly land to people who were once their allies and comrades in arms.

'Consider: when Pausanius buried them he thought he was laying them in a friendly land and among friends. But if you put us to death and make the territory of Plataea a Theban province will you not be leaving them in a hostile land and among their murderers — these, your fathers and kinsmen and deprived of the honours they now enjoy? These things are not consistent with your honour because they sided with the enemies of the Spartans.'

Thucydides then records the speech of the Theban envoys who addressed the judges at length. The Thebans belittled the efforts of the Plataeans against the Persians and their motives for fighting the Persians. They denied that they had made an unprovoked attack on the city.

'The judges them summoned the Plataeans to appear before them one by one and put to them the same question as before. Had they done anything in the present war to help the Spartans? Those who answered 'No' were taken away and slain. The number of the Plataeans who perished was not less than two hundred and of the Athenians, twenty-five. The women were sold as slaves.'

7

Pylos

When the Athenian fleet arrived off the coast of Laconia and news reached it that the Peloponnesian fleet was already in Corcyra, Eurymedon and Sophocles were for pressing on to Corcyra but Demosthenes urged them to put in at Pylos, do what had to be done there and afterwards continue the voyage to Corcyra. They objected, but as luck would have it a storm blew up and carried the fleet to Pylos. Demosthenes at once urged them to fortify the place and it was for this purpose he had sailed with them. He pointed out that there was no lack of timber and stone on the site. The position was naturally a strong one. Not only was Pylos itself unoccupied but so was the country in the immediate neighbourhood: Pylos is about four hundred stadia from Sparta. It lies in the land that used to be Messenia; the Lacedaemonians now call it Coryphasium. The other two generals said there were plenty of other unoccupied headlands in the Peloponnese which Demosthenes could seize if he wished to put the city to expense. But Demosthenes thought that Pylos had special advantage over other headlands; there was a harbour close by and the Messenians who originally owned the land and spoke the same dialect as the Lacedaemonians, could do the enemy much harm if they used it as a base for operation and at the same time would provide a trustworthy garrison for it.

But Demosthenes could not prevail on the other two generals nor on the soldiers to accept his view, nor yet the divisional commanders whom he later tried to win over. Since the weather was unfavourable for sailing the army hung about doing nothing. The soldiers got bored and wanting something to do set about fortifying the place. They had no iron tools for stone-working so they just picked up stones and put them together as they fitted. Where mortar was needed, for lack of hods they carried it on their backs bending over in such a position as to make it stay in place, clasping both hands behind them. They worked at great speed so that they could complete the fortification of the most vulnerable parts before the Lacedaemonians came out against them, for the greater part of the site was so strong by nature that it had no need for a wall. As for the Lacedaemonians they were celebrating a festival when a report reached them about the activities of the Athenians at Pylos. They made light of the report thinking that if they took to the field the Athenians would withdraw, or, if not, they could easily take the place by force. No doubt they were influenced too by the fact that their army was in Attica. It took the Athenians six days to complete the wall on the land side and at other points which needed strengthening. The Athenians then left Demosthenes there with five ships to defend the place. The main part of the fleet then proceeded on its way to Corcyra and Sicily.

But the Peloponnesians who were in Attica, when they learned that the Athenians had occupied Pylos, returned home in haste for King Agis and the Lacedaemonians thought the operations at Pylos were of grave concern to them. Moreover they had made their invasion early in the year when the grain was still green and most of the divisions were short of food; also bad weather which came on with storms of greater violence than was to be expected so late in the spring discomfited the army.

On the return of the Peloponnesians from Attica, the Spartans themselves and the Perioeci who were in the neighbourhood of Pylos at once came to the relief of Pylos. Word was sent round to the states of the Peloponnesus bidding them come to the relief of Pylos as quickly as possible. But before the Peloponnesian fleet had reached Pylos, Demosthenes sent out two ships to inform Eurymedon and the Athenian fleet that they should come at once to his aid as their position on Pylos was in danger. The fleet proceeded in haste to meet Demosthenes' call for help. Meanwhile the Lacedaemonians were busy with their preparation both by land and by sea and they expected to have no difficulty in capturing a fortification which had been constructed hastily and was occupied by only a few men. They expected the Athenian fleet to arrive soon and it was their intention in case they should fail to take the place before the arrival of the Athenian fleet, to block up the entrances to the harbour and thus make it impossible for the Athenians to anchor inside the harbour.

Now the island called Sphacteria extends along the mainland and lies quite close to it thus making the harbour safe and the entrances to it narrow; on one side, opposite the Athenian fortifications and Pylos there is only space for two ships to pass through, while on the other side, next to the other part of the mainland there is space for eight or nine. The whole island was thickly wooded and since it was uninhabited had no roads or tracks. Its length was about fifteen stadia.

The Lacedaemonians' intention was to close up tightly both entrances to the harbour by means of ships with their prows facing outward. As for the island, they were afraid that the Athenians might use it as a base for operations against them. They conveyed some Hoplites across, at the same time posting others along the mainland. By these measures, they thought, the Athenians would find not only the island hostile to them but also the mainland since this had no landing places, for there were no harbours along the shore of Pylos outside the entrance on the side towards the sea and therefore the Athenians would have no base from which they could aid their countrymen. Consequently the Lacedaemonians believed that without running the risk of a sea battle they could probably reduce the place by siege since it had been occupied at short notice and was not supplied with provisions. As soon as they reached this conclusion they transported the Hoplites to the island choosing them by lot from the various companies. Several detachments had before this time crossed over, one group relieving another, the last to do so — and this is the force that was captured, numbering four hundred and twenty, in addition to the Helots who accompanied them. They were commanded by Epitadas, son of Molobrus.

Meanwhile Demosthenes, seeing that the Lacedaemonians intended to attack him by sea and by land at the same time, made his own preparations. He drew ashore close under the fortification the triremes that remained to him of those that had been left in his charge and built a stockade round them. He then armed their crews with shields — rather poor ones, most of them made of plaited willow, for it was not possible to procure arms in uninhabited country, and such as they took from a thirty-oared privateer belonging to some Messenians who chanced to come along and among them were about forty Hoplites whom Demosthenes enrolled among his own men.

Demosthenes then posted the greater part of his troops — the unarmed and the armed — at the best fortified and stronger parts of the place on the side facing the mainland — giving them orders to ward off any attack by the enemy's infantry if it should attack. He himself selected from the whole body of his troops sixty Hoplites and a few archers and sallied out from the fort to the point on the sea-shore where he thought the enemy would be most likely to attempt a landing. The ground was indeed difficult and rocky where it faced the sea, yet since the Athenian wall was weakest at this point the enemy, he thought, would be only too eager to make an assault there; in fact the Athenians had left the wall weak at this point because they never expected to be defeated at sea and Demosthenes knew that if the enemy could force a landing at this point the place could be easily taken. Accordingly he posted his Hoplites at this point, bringing them to the very edge of the sea, determined to ward off the enemy if he could. He then addressed them in this way:

'Soldiers, my comrades in this present danger, let no one of you in this moment of necessity seek to demonstrate his intelligence by calculating the full extent of the danger that threatens us. Let him rather face the enemy with unreflecting confidence that he will survive these perils. For whenever it comes as now to a case of necessity, there is no room for reflection and calculation; what is needed is to accept the hazard without hesitation. However, as I see the situation, the odds are on our side, if we are resolved to stand our ground and are not so struck with fear of their numbers that we throw away the advantages of our position. As regards the position, the difficulty of approach I regard as a point in our favour since if we stand firm that becomes an advantage to us, but if we give way, even though the ground be rough, it will be easy of access if there is no resistance from us. And we shall then find the enemy more formidable since it will not be an easy matter for them to turn and withdraw if hard pressed by us. For though they can easily be repelled while on board their ships, once they have landed they are on an equal footing with us. As regards their numbers we should not be excessively afraid; for they will have to fight in small detachments owing to the difficulty of bringing their ships to the shore. We do not have to face an army which is fighting on land under similar conditions as our own, but fighting on ships, and these require many favourable circumstances when they are on the sea. I therefore consider that their disadvantages counterbalance our inferiority in numbers. At the same time I call upon you who are Athenians and who know from experience that it is not possible to make a landing on a defended shore if the defenders stand firm and do not give way through fear of the splashing oars and the terrifying appearance of ships bearing down upon them. I call upon you, now in your turn to stand firm and warding off the enemy at the very water's edge save yourselves and our stronghold.'

The encouragement from Demosthenes made the Athenians even more confident and going right down to the water's edge they took up their positions at the very brink of the sea.

For their part the Lacedaemonians moved forward and attacked the fortification both by land and with their ships which numbered forty-three, the admiral in charge of the fleet being Thrasymelidas, son of Cratesicles, a Spartan. He attacked just where Demosthenes had expected. The Athenians defended themselves from attack by land and by sea. But the enemy divided their ships into small groups because there was not space for a larger number to approach the shore. Each group rested in turn and then charged upon the Athenians showing great enthusiasm and cheering each other on in their determination to force the enemy back and take the fortification. Brasidas showed himself most conspicuous of all. Being captain of a galley he noticed that the captains and steersmen, because the shore was rocky, hesitated and tried to spare their ships even when it seemed possible to make a landing, for fear of dashing their ships to pieces on the rocks. Brasidas kept shouting at them that it was most improper of them, out of a desire to save some timber, to allow the enemy to hold a fort they had built in Lacedaemonian country; they must break their ships in order to force a landing. The allies he bade, in return for great benefits received from the Lacedaemonians, not to shrink from making them a free gift of their ships in the present emergency, but to run them aground, get ashore in any way they could and overcome all resistance. He not only urged on the rest in this way but compelled his own helmsman to beach his ship. He made for the gangway but in trying to step ashore was knocked back by the Athenians, and, after receiving many wounds, collapsed. As he fell into the forward part of the ship, his shield slipped off into the sea. It was carried ashore and picked up by Athenians who afterwards used it as a trophy which they set up to commemorate this attack.

After making attacks that day and part of the next, the Peloponnesians ceased their assaults. On the third day they sent some of their ships to Asine for wood with which to make siege engines hoping that by means of these engines they would be able to take the part of the wall opposite the harbour, in spite of its height since here it was quite practicable to make a landing. Meanwhile the Athenian fleet from Zacynthus arrived; it now numbered fifty ships. When they saw that both the mainland and the island were full of Hoplites and that the Lacedaemonian ships were in the harbour and not preparing to come out, they, being at a loss where to anchor, made, for the present, to Prote an uninhabited island not far from Pylos and bivouacked there. The next day they set sail, having first made preparations to give battle in case the enemy should come out into the open to meet them; if not they intended to sail into the harbour themselves.

The Lacedaemonians did not put out to confront the Athenians. Somehow they had failed to block up the entrance as they had intended to do. They remained inactive on the shore putting their equipment in order and making ready in case anyone sailed into the harbour to fight there for there was plenty of room. As for the Athenians, when they saw the situation, they rushed in upon them by both entrances and falling upon their ships most of which were now afloat and facing forward, put them to flight and giving chase as far as the short distance allowed, not only damaged many of them but captured five, one of them with all her crew. The rest they kept on ramming even after they had fled to the safety of the shore. Others were cut to pieces while still being manned before they could put to sea. Some they took in tow empty, their crews having taken flight, and began to haul them away. At this sight the Lacedaemonian soldiers on the shore overwhelmed with grief at the impending calamity in that their comrades on the island were being cut off hastened to the rescue and wading into the sea in full armour seized hold of the ships and tried to pull them

46

back. Each man felt that no progress was being made where he himself was not present to help. The tumult that arose was terrific.

Finally after inflicting grave injuries on each other and doing much damage the two sides separated, the Lacedaemonians saving all their empty ships except those which had been taken at first. Both sides then returned to their camps. The Athenians then set up a trophy, and gave back the dead. They seized hold of the wrecks and immediately began to sail round the island and keep it under guard, regarding the men on it as now cut off. On the other hand the Peloponnesans on the mainland and the reinforcements which had now arrived from all directions remained in position at Pylos.

At Sparta when news was received of what had happened at Pylos it was regarded as a disaster. It was decided that the magistrates should go down to the camp, see the situation and then decide what should be done. When these saw that no help could be given to the men on the island and at the same time they were unwilling to run the risk of their being starved to death or be forced to submit to superior numbers, they decided, so far as Pylos was concerned, to make a truce with the Athenian generals, if they were willing and to send envoys to Athens to try to reach an agreement and thus recover their men as quickly as possible.

The generals consented and a truce was drawn up on the following terms:

The Lacedaemonians were to surrender to the Athenians the ships in which they had fought the battle and were to bring to Pylos and surrender all the other ships of war which they had in Laconia.

The Lacedaemonians were not to attack the fortification by sea or by land.

The Athenians were to permit the Lacedaemonians on the mainland to send flour to the men on the island, a fixed amount and already kneaded, for each soldier two quarts of barley meal and a pint of wine and a ration of meat and for each servant half as much and they were to send these things to the island under the supervision of the Athenians and no boat was to go there secretly.

The Athenians were to go on guarding the island as before but without landing on it and were not to attack the army of the Peloponnesians by sea or by land.

If either party were to violate this agreement, the truce should forthwith be at an end.

The truce was to hold good until the Lacedaemonian envoys got back and the Athenians were to convey them there in a trireme and bring them back.

On their return this truce was to be at an end and the Athenians were to restore the ships in as good a condition as when they received them.

The truce was concluded on these terms: the ships, sixty in number, were delivered.

When they arrived at Athens the Spartan envoys spoke to the Assembly: Thucydides gives us in full the address of the envoys. They began by reminding the Athenians that the fortunes of war swing now this way, now that. Athens had had a stroke of good fortune at Pylos. She should take the opportunity to come to generous terms with Sparta before Athens suffered a stroke of ill fortune. The envoys suggested that the men on the island be released and in return Sparta would cease making war on Athens and sign a treaty of friendship.

Under the influence of the demagogue Cleon the Assembly rejected the Spartan proposal.

The Spartan envoys then suggested that a small group be formed consisting of themselves and a few Athenian representatives to discuss a possible agreement in private rather than openly in the Assembly. Cleon rejected this suggestion saying that if the Spartans had honest proposals to make they should not object to their being debated openly in the Assembly.

The Athenians were then persuaded by Cleon to put forward their own proposals which were that:

The men on the island must first give up themselves and their arms and be brought to Athens. On their arrival at Athens the Lacedaemonians must give back Nisea, Pegae, Troezen and Achaea, which had not been taken in war but had been ceded by the Athenians in an agreement made sometime before as a result of misfortunes. They could then recover the men and make a treaty for so long as both sides agreed.

To these proposals the envoys made no response but requested the appointment of Athenian commissioners who should confer with them and after a full consideration of all the details should agree on such terms as both parties could approve. Cleon then attacked them in violent language saying that he had known before this that they had no honourable intentions and now it was clear since they were unwilling to speak out before the people but wanted to meet a few men in conference. He bade them if their purpose was honest to speak out before them all. But the Lacedaemonians seeing that it was impossible to announce in full assembly such concessions as they might think it best to make in view of their present misfortune lest they lose face with their allies if they proposed them and were rebuffed, and seeing also that the Athenians would not grant their proposals on acceptable conditions withdrew from Athens, having failed to accomplish their mission.

On the return of the envoys to Pylos the truce came to an immediate end. The Lacedaemonians asked for the return of their ships as stipulated in the agreement but the Athenians accused them of having made an attack on the fort, and other acts which hardly seem worth mentioning, and refused to give up the ships, strongly arguing that it had been agreed that if there was any violation of the truce whatever, it became void. The Lacedaemonians protested that they were the victims of gross injustice. They went away and renewed hostilities. The Athenians kept sailing round the island by day with two ships going in opposite directions and at night their whole fleet lay at anchor on all sides of it, except to seaward when there was a wind. Twenty additional ships came from Athens to assist them in the blockade, so that they now had seventy in all. As for the Peloponnesians they remained in camp on the mainland, continually making attacks on the fort, on the look-out for any opportunity of rescuing their men.

The blockade of the island began to be very troublesome to the Athenians on account of the lack of food and of water. For there was only one spring on Pylos, on the top of the acropolis and that was only a small spring. The soldiers, for the most part, scraped away the shingle on the beach and drank such water as you might expect to find there. What added to their discomfort was the very confined space available for bivouacking. Since there was no anchorage for the ships their crew took their meals ashore while the rest of the fleet lay at anchor out at sea. Great discouragement too was caused by the surprising length of the siege. The Athenians had hoped that with the men being on a desert island with only brackish water to drink they would hold out for only a few days. What enabled men to survive much longer was the measures taken by the Lacedaemonians to supply the men with food. They had called for volunteers to take to the island ground corn, wine, cheese and other foods such as might be serviceable under siege conditions. Large rewards were offered and freedom was promised to any Helot who could get food in. Many took the risks involved, especially the Helots, putting out from many places along the coast and approaching the island by night from the seaward side. If possible they waited for a wind to carry them to the shore, for they found it easier to elude the guard of triremes when the wind was blowing from the sea, since then it was impossible for the ships to lie at their moorings off the island, while they themselves ran ashore regardless of consequences, since a value had been set upon the boats which they drove upon the beach and the Hoplites would be on watch for them at the landing places on the island. All, however, who made the attempt in calm weather were captured. At the harbour too there were divers who swam underwater to the island towing by a cord skins filled with poppy seed mixed with honey and bruised linseed. At first they were not discovered but afterwards watches were set for them. And so both sides tried every device, the one side to get food into the island, the other to catch them doing it.

Meanwhile in Athens, when they heard that their army was in difficulties and that food was reaching the men on the island they were perplexed and began to fear that winter would overtake them while they were still engaged in the blockade. For they saw that the conveyance of supplies round the Peloponnesus in winter would be impossible since there were no harbours in the neighbourhood. The result would be a failure of the blockade. Either their own troops would become less vigilant and permit some of the men to escape or else, waiting for bad weather they would sail away in the boats that brought them food. What especially caused alarm was the attitude of the Lacedaemonians. It was felt that as they were no longer making overtures for a settlement they must have some good reasons for confidence. The Athenians began to regret having rejected their previous proposals for a settlement. Cleon, recognizing that their hostility was directed against him because he had prevented the settlement proposal earlier, said that the messengers from Pylos were not telling the truth about the situation there, whereupon the messengers advised that if their own account of the situation at Pylos was not believed, commissioners be appointed to visit Pylos and bring back a report. The Athenians chose Cleon himself as one of the Commissioners, with Theagenes as his colleague. Cleon now saw that he was in a difficult position. It would be embarrassing for him if he had to report that the account given by the messengers was correct but if he reported otherwise he might be proved to be a liar. So he told the Assembly that it was a waste of time to send commissioners. If they believed the messengers' reports they should send a fleet to Pylos with orders to capture the men on the island. Then pointing at Nicias, son of Niceratus one of the generals and a personal enemy of Cleon's, Cleon told the Assembly that it would be an easy matter to capture the men on the island if the generals were men and that is what he would have done had he been in command.

An uproar broke out in the Assembly. People asked him why he did not sail now if he thought it an easy matter to take the men on the island. Nicias, noticing the way the debate was developing and still smarting under Cleon's taunt told him that as far as the generals were concerned he could take whatever force he wished and make the attempt. At first Cleon showed himself willing to accept this challenge for he did not believe that Nicias would really hand over command to him. When he realized that Nicias was serious and wished to surrender the command to him Cleon began to back out saying that Nicias, not he, Cleon, was in command. But again Nicias urged him to sail and called upon the people to witness that he offered to resign his command. At length Cleon seeing that he had no alternative, said he would sail and sail without taking any Athenian soldiers. He came forward and said he was not afraid of the Lacedaemonians and all he would take with him were some Lemnian and Imbrian archers who happened to be in Athens together with a body of slingers who had come from Aenus and four hundred archers from other places.

Given this force he promised that within twenty days he would bring back the men on the island alive or slay them on the spot. This boast aroused laughter but sensible men in the Assembly were glad because they saw that one of two good things would ensue. Either they would get rid of Cleon — which they would prefer — or he would subdue the Lacedaemonians on their behalf.

So arrangements were made and a vote taken in the Assembly. Cleon then chose as his colleague, Demosthenes, one of the generals at Pylos. He chose Demosthenes because he had heard that Demosthenes was planning to make an assault on the island and that the soldiers who were living in very cramped and uncomfortable conditions were eager to accept the risk of an attack.

Demosthenes himself had been encouraged by a fire which swept the island. The soldiers had so little living room that they were obliged to land on the edge of the island in order to take their meals, setting a guard to keep watch while they ate. One of the men having a meal in these circumstances accidentally set fire to the forest. A breeze sprang up and before they knew it the whole forest was burnt down. Demosthenes now saw that the island was less difficult for making a landing than he had thought.

Cleon meanwhile had sent on word to Demosthenes that he would soon arrive, bringing the force for which he had asked. As soon as the army already with Demosthenes, and the troops brought by Cleon, had joined up, they sent a herald to the enemy's camp on the mainland, giving them the opportunity, if they wished to avoid a conflict, to order the men on the island to surrender themselves and their arms and be held in a mild form of custody until a settlement could be reached on the wider issues.

This offer being rejected the Athenians waited for one day. On the next day, while it was still dark, they embarked all the Hoplites in a few vessels a little before dawn; they numbered about eight hundred. They landed them on both sides of the island — on the seaward side and on the side facing the harbour. The Hoplites immediately advanced at the double to the first guard post on the island. For the forces of the enemy were disposed as follows: in this first post there were about thirty Hoplites. The central and most level part of the island where their water-supply was located, was held by the main body of troops under Epitadas. A small detachment guarded the northern tip of the island opposite Pylos. This point was precipitous on the side facing the sea and least assailable toward the land. Such then was the disposition of the enemy's forces.

The Athenians charged at full speed on the men in the first

guard post and slew them all for most were either still in bed or getting on their armour. They had not noticed the Athenian ships supposing that they were engaged on routine patrol. With the coming of dawn the rest of the army began to disembark. They were the crews of slightly more than seventy ships, each equipped in his own way besides eight hundred archers and the same number of slingers, as well as the Messenians who had come to reinforce them and all the others on duty around Pylos except those left to guard the fort. Demosthenes divided them into companies of about two hundred men each. They occupied the highest points in the island, so that the Lacedaemonians wherever they took up their position were surrounded by enemy above them. They would also find that whichever way they moved they had the Athenians' lightly armed troops in their rear to harass them. At the same time the Hoplites did not advance against them. If the Athenians' lightly armed troops approached them too closely the Lacedaemonians would drive them away but the lightly armed men would then wheel round and attack them from the rear or flank. Being so lightly equipped they could move about on the rough terrain quickly and with ease. The Lacedaemonians, wearing heavy armour, were unable to pursue them over the rough ground.

After this skirmishing had been going on for some time the Lacedaemonians being heavily equipped, were unable to dash out with the same speed as before. The lightly armed troops finding that the enemy now fought with less vigour became more confident. They could see for themselves that they outnumbered the Lacedaemonians. They were now familiar with the Lacedaemonians' way of fighting and found them less terrible than they had expected when they first realized that they were to fight the dreaded Lacedaemonians. Their fear was replaced by a feeling that they were equal to the enemy or superior to him. They now all together rushed upon the Lacedaemonians pelting them with stones, darts, arrows and anything else that came to hand. The shouting which accompanied this onslaught confounded the Lacedaemonians, not being used to such warfare. Dust rose from the newly burnt wood and it was impossible to see in front of one with the arrows and stones flying through clouds of dust from the hands of numerous assailants. The Lacedaemonians now found themselves engaged in a rough sort of fighting. Their caps could not keep out the arrows, darts broke off in their armour and they could not launch an attack for they could not see what was in front of them and they were unable to hear words of command because of the hubbub made by the enemy. Danger surrounded them on every side and there seemed no way of escape.

At last when the Lacedaemonians saw that many of their men were wounded, they closed ranks and fell back to the furthermost fortification on the island where they had a small garrison. But the moment they began to fall back the light-armed troops, now more confident, charged forward with an even louder cry. Some of the Lacedaemonians in the retreat were slain but most managed to reach the fort in safety. The Athenians attacked them in the fort but both sides held out.

At last the general of the Messenians came to Cleon and asked to be given some of the archers and light-armed troops so that he could get round in the enemy's rear. He was given what he asked for and starting from a point out of sight from the enemy suddenly appeared on the high ground above the enemy to their consternation and the joy of the Athenian force. The Lacedaemonians were now assaulted from all sides and began to give way. Cleon and Demosthenes seeing that the enemy might be annihilated held back their own men, wishing to deliver them alive to the Athenians. So they proclaimed by a herald that the Lacedaemonians might if they wished surrender themselves and their army to the Athenians who would decide what to do with them. When the Lacedaemonians heard this most of them lowered their shields and waved their hands indicating that they accepted the terms proposed. The next day the Athenians distributed the prisoners and the various triremes and set off for Athens. The Athenians and Peloponnesians now withdrew from Pylos and returned home with their respective forces.

Of all the events of this war, this came as the greatest surprise to the Hellenic world; for men could not conceive that the Lacedaemonians would be forced by hunger or any other compulsion to give up their arms but believed they would keep them till they died. When the captives were brought to Athens, the Athenians resolved to keep them in prison until some agreement could be reached but if the Peloponnesians were to invade their land, they would take out the captives and kill them. . . .

The Athenians also placed a garrison in Pylos, and the Messenians at Naupactus, regarding the territory as their fatherland — for Pylos belongs to the country that was once Messenia — sent thither such of their own number as were fitted for the task and proceeded to ravage the Laconian territory, and they did a great deal of damage for the Lacedaemonians had never before experienced warfare of this sort. When the Helots began to desert and there was reason to fear that the insurrection might make even further headway they were uneasy.

8

Mytilene and the Two Triremes

Mytilene, the largest city in the island of Lesbos, was a tribute-paying dependent ally of Athens, enjoying a rather favourable status. In the fourth year of the war, instigated by Sparta, Mytilene revolted. The Athenians sent a strong force under the command of Paches to put down the rebellion. A Spartan named Salaethus managed to slip into the city with the news that a Spartan fleet was on its way. The Spartan fleet was delayed.

Thucydides records what then took place:

The Mytilenaeans seeing that the Spartan fleet did not arrive and was loitering on the way, and that food in the city was exhausted, were compelled to seek terms with the Athenians.

The Spartan Salaethus, who no longer expected the fleet to arrive, equipped the common people with heavy armour and weapons so that they could fight the Athenian troops. But the people, now armed, ordered the authorities to hand over to them all existing stocks of food, otherwise, they said, they would themselves come to terms with the Athenians. Under this threat the authorities together with the armed commons made an agreement with the Athenians, allowing the Athenians to decide on the fate of the Mytilenaeans, who were permitted to send envoys to Athens to state their case.

The Peloponnesian fleet arrived off Mytilene one week after the city had capitulated. It at once returned home.

Paches caught Salaethus and sent him and those whom he regarded as ringleaders of the revolt to Athens; at the same time he asked for instructions for what he should do with the other Mytilenaeans who had revolted and then surrendered.

The Athenians at once put Salaethus to death and held a

meeting of the Assembly to decide what to do with the people of Mytilene who had surrendered to Paches. The Assembly met in a mood of intense anger against Mytilene. What contributed to their anger was the fact that a Peloponnesian fleet had managed to get across to Ionia without being intercepted. This seemed to suggest that the revolt had been carefully planned. The Assembly voted that every adult man in Mytilene should be put to death, and the women and children sold into slavery.

A trireme was immediately despatched with instructions to Paches that he should carry out the decision of the Assembly without delay.

On the following morning in Athens there was a revulsion of feeling against the decision reached on the previous day. To many it seemed cruel and outrageous that not merely those responsible for the revolt should be punished, but everyone in the city. The Mytilenaean envoys, aware of this change of sentiment, got together with their sympathizers and persuaded the authorities to hold another debate on the Mytilenaean question.

At the second debate Cleon, son of Cleaenetus, who in the first debate had successfully pressed for the death penalty for all adult males in the city, spoke again. He was the most violent of the citizens and carried a lot of influence in the Assembly.

Thucydides gives Cleon's speech in full. After expressing his contempt for those who wished to re-open an issue already decided Cleon told the Assembly that the allies and dependants of Athens remained loyal not from goodwill or gratitude to Athens but solely out of fear of her superior strength. Athens must demonstrate her strength by severely punishing those who offended her. It was wrong to blame only the aristocratic party and exonerate the party of the common people. Both parties had united to attack Athens and there were no mitigating circumstances in favour of Mytilene. The city was strongly fortified and had no grounds for fearing an attack by the enemies of Athens. An attack could only come from the sea and Mytilene had a fleet of triremes to defend her under her own control.

Athens should punish the Mytilenaeans in a way which would deter any others contemplating revolt.

The next speaker was Diodotus, son of Eucrates, who in the previous day's debate had spoken against putting to death all adult males in Mytilene.

In the account of his speech given by Thucydides Diodotus said that if death was the penalty for those who revolted and resisted to the end as well as for those who having revolted regretted their action and surrendered no rebels in future would ever surrender. They would resist to the end, causing Athens much loss and trouble. Leniency should be shown to those who having revolted regretted their action and capitulated.

It would be a mistake too to treat the populace, who were usually on the side of Athens, in the same way as the aristocracy were treated. If this were done the populace in any future revolt would act together with the aristocrats.

Thucydides writes:

'Such was the speech of Diodotus. After these opinions had been expressed with nearly equal force the one against the other, it seemed that opinions were almost equally divided. But when a vote was taken the view of Diodotus prevailed. The authorities then immediately despatched a second trireme with all haste, hoping that the first trireme which had the start of about a day and a night might not arrive first in which case the second trireme would on arrival find that the executions had already taken place. The Mytilenaean envoys provided wine and barley to the crew and promised a large reward if they should arrive in time. Such was their haste on the voyage that they kept on rowing as they ate their barley cakes, kneaded with wine and oil and took turns at sleeping and rowing. By good fortune no contrary wind arose and since the earlier ship had no reason to hurry on so miserable a mission although the first trireme did in fact arrive first. Paches had only time enough to read the decree and was about to carry out the orders when the second trireme pulled in and so saved the inhabitants. By just so much did Mytilene escape its peril.

9

Civil Strife in Corcyra

The Corcyraeans had been engaged in civil strife ever since the home-coming of the captives taken in the two sea-fights off Epdiamnus, who had been released by the Corinthians. Nominally they had been set free on bail of eight hundred talents pledged by their consuls. In fact they had been bribed to bring Corcyra over to the Corinthian side. These men had been going from citizen to citizen intriguing with them with the aim of inducing the city to revolt from Athens. Then an Attic and a Corinthian vessel arrived each bringing envoys. After the envoys had stated their case, the Corcyraeans voted to continue to be allies of Athens in accordance with their agreement. At the same time they wished to renew their former friendship with the Peloponnesians. Thereupon the returned prisoners brought Peithias, a volunteer consul of the Athenians and leader of the popular party, to trial, accusing him of trying to bring Corcyra into submission to Athens. But he was acquitted and then in turn brought law suits against the five richest men of their party alleging that they were cutting down vine-crops from the sacred precincts of Zeus and Alcinous, an offence for which a fine of a stater for each stake was fixed by law. They were convicted and because of the very large amount of the fine took refuge in the temples as suppliants that they might arrange to pay the fine by instalments. Peithias, who was a member of the Council persuaded the Council to let the law take its course. The convicted men, seeing that they were prevented by the law from carrying out their intentions and learning that Peithias so long as he remained a member of the Council would continue in his efforts to persuade the people to conclude an offensive and defensive alliance with Athens got together and rushing into the Council chamber with daggers in their hands killed Peithias and others, both members of Council and others, to the number of sixty. A few, however, who held the same political views as Peithias managed to escape by taking refuge in the Attic trireme which was still in the harbour.

After they had acted in this way the conspirators called together the Corcyraeans and told them that everything was for the best. Now they were least likely to be subjugated by the Athenians and in future they should remain neutral and refuse to receive either party in this case arriving with more than one vessel, regarding more than one vessel as indicating a hostile intent. Having thus spoken they compelled the people to ratify their purpose. They also sent at once envoys to Athens to explain recent events at Corcyra and to persuade the Corcyraean refugees in Athens to do nothing which might lead the Athenians to take hostile action against Corcyra. But when the envoys arrived the Athenians arrested them on a charge of having revolutionary intentions and sent them to Aegina in custody.

Meanwhile the party in Corcyra who were now in a dominant position (i.e. the oligarchs), on the arrival of a Corinthian trireme with Lacedaemonian envoys, attacked the populace and were victorious in the fight. When night came on, the people took refuge in the Acropolis and other high places. There they banded themselves together and established themselves securely. They held also the Hyllaic harbour while the other party seized the district of the market-place, where many of them lived, and the nearby harbour, which faces the mainland.

On the next day the two sides clashed occasionally and both sides sent emissaries into the fields calling on the slaves to aid them and promising them their freedom. Most of the slaves went to the aid of the popular party while the other party obtained the support of eight hundred mercenaries from the mainland.

After a day's interval another fight took place and the popular party won as they had the advantage of the strength of their position as well as of their numbers. The women also boldly joined in the fight, throwing tiles from the houses and enduring the uproar with a courage beyond their sex.

About sunset the oligarchs, now on the run, fearing that the democrats might by a sudden rush seize the arsenal and put all the oligarchs to the sword, set fire to the dwelling houses round the market place and to the tenement blocks, so as to prevent an attack, sparing neither their own houses nor those of others. The result was that much property was destroyed by fire and if a wind had sprung up the whole city would have been in danger of being burnt down. During the night after they had ceased fighting both parties rested but remained on the alert. Now that the people's party was in a dominant position, the Corinthian ship slipped out of the harbour. Many of the mercenaries were conveyed over to the mainland, unobserved.

On the following day Nicostratus, son of Diitrephes, general of the Athenians, arrived with twelve ships and five hundred Messenian Hoplites. He tried to negotiate a settlement between the factions and succeeded in persuading them to come to an agreement: that the twelve men who were chiefly to blame should be brought to trial (these men immediately left the country) and the rest should make peace with each other and enter into a defensive and offensive alliance with Athens. When he had concluded these arrangements he was about to sail away but the leaders of the democratic party persuaded him to leave with them five of his ships that their opponents might be less inclined to make trouble; they agreed on their part to man and send with him an equal number of their own ships. He agreed and they began to choose their personal enemies to man the ships. But these men, who were afraid of being sent to Athens, sat down at the Temple of Dioscuri as suppliants. Nicostratus offered them guarantees and spoke re-assuringly to them, but without effect. The democratic party on this refusal armed themselves and would have slain any oligarchs whom they chanced to meet had not Nicostratus restrained them. The others seeing what was going on, sat down in the Temple of Hera as suppliants: they were not less than four hundred in number. The democrats fearing that they might start a revolution, persuaded them to rise and conveyed them to the island which lies opposite the Temple of Hera. They provided them with provisions regularly.

At this point in the civil strife, on the fourth or fifth day after the transfer of the men to the island, the Peloponnesian ships arrived from Cyllene where they had been lying since their voyage from Ionia: they numbered fifty-three. Alcidas was in command as before, with Brasidas accompanying him as adviser. They came to anchor first at Sybota, a harbour on the mainland and there crossed to Corcyra. The democratic party, now in

61

control in Corcyra, was thrown into confusion by these events. They were in a state of panic about the situation in Corcyra. They proceeded to equip sixty ships and to send them out against the enemy as fast as they were manned although the Athenians asked that they be permitted to sail out first and the Corcyraean vessels sail out later in a body. When the Corcyraean ships sailed out, two of them immediately deserted to the enemy while in the other ships there was fighting among the crews. There was disorder among the Corcyraean fleet.

When the Peloponnesians saw the confusion in the Corcyraean fleet they arrayed only twenty ships against the Corcyraeans and set all the rest against the twelve Athenian ships which included the Salaminia and the Paralos.

Now the Corcyraeans, since they were attacking in bad order with only a few ships at a time, were having trouble in their part of the battle and the Athenians, fearing the enemy's superior numbers and seeing the danger of being surrounded, did not attack the whole body together nor the centre of the fleet arrayed against them, but rushed upon one of the wings and sank a single ship. When the Peloponnesians, after this manoeuvre formed their ships in a circle, the Athenians kept sailing round the Peloponnesian fleet trying to throw it into disorder. But those who were facing the Corcyraeans, fearing a repetition of what happened at Naupactus, came to the rescue, and the whole fleet, now united, advanced simultaneously upon the Athenians. The Athenians then began to withdraw, backing water and hoping that the Corcyraean ships might, as far as possible, withdraw into the harbour as they themselves retired slowly and the enemy's attacks were directed solely against them. Such then was the course of the battle, which lasted until sunset.

The Corcyraeans, afraid that the enemy, now in a dominant position, might sail against the city and either take on board the prisoners on the island or commit some other hostile act removed these prisoners once again to the Temple of Hera and then did what they could to protect the city. The Peloponnesians however, in spite of their victory in the naval battle, did not dare to attack the city but with thirteen Corcyraean ships which they had captured sailed back to the harbour on the mainland from which they had set out. On the following day they were still disinclined to attack the city although the inhabitants were in a state of panic and though Brasidas, it is said, urged Alcidas to attack the city but did not have equal authority with him. Instead they merely landed at Leucimne and destroyed the crops.

Meanwhile the popular party in Corcyra, becoming alarmed that the enemy ships might attack them conferred with the suppliants and other members of the opposite party about the best way to save the city. They persuaded some of them to go aboard the ships, for in spite of all that had happened the Corcyraeans still had thirty ships ready for manning. But the Peloponnesians after ravaging the land until mid-day, sailed away. Just before night-fall a signal was flashed to them that sixty Athenian ships were approaching from Leucas. These ships under the command of Eurymedon, son of Thucles, had been despatched by the Athenians when they learnt about the civil strife in Corcyra and that a fleet under Alcidas was about to sail for Corcyra.

The Peloponnesians accordingly set sail for home that very night, travelling at top speed and hugging the coast. They hauled their ships across the Leucadian isthmus, to avoid being seen. As soon as the Corcyraeans realized that the Athenian fleet was approaching and the enemy fleet had left, secretly brought into the city the Messenians, who had until then been outside the walls and ordered the ships to sail round into the Hyllaic harbour and while these were on their way they slew any of their personal enemies whom they could lay their hands on. They also killed as soon as they disembarked all those whom they had persuaded to go aboard the ships. They then went to the Temple of Hera, persuaded about fifty of the suppliants to come out and stand trial. Those they condemned to death. But most of the suppliants, not having consented to come to trial, as soon as they saw what was happening began to destroy one another within the sacred precincts. A few hanged themselves from trees while others took their lives by the best available means. And during the seven days that Eurymedon stayed there after his arrival with the sixty ships, the Corcyraeans slaughtered such of their fellow citizens whom they considered to be personal enemies. The charge they brought was that of conspiring to overthrow the democracy but some were despatched purely on grounds of personal enmity. Others were slain because money was owing to them, by those who had borrowed it. Every form of death took place and such horrors as are apt to occur in such circumstances — and even worse. For father slew son, men were dragged from temples and slain nearby and some were even walled up in the Temple of Dionysus and perished there.

To such outrageous conduct did civil strife lead and it seemed the more outrageous because it was among the first to occur for afterwards practically the whole Greek world was involved. For in each State the leaders of the democratic parties were in dispute with the oligarchs, the former seeking to bring in the Athenians and the latter seeking to bring in the Lacedaemonians. And in time of peace there would have been no grounds for bringing in foreign intervention — and little inclination to do so. But now that Athens and the Lacedaemonians were at war either faction in the various Greek cities found it easy if it desired a revolution to call in allies for the discomfiture of its opponents and the strengthening of its own cause. And so there fell upon the cities of Greece because of revolutions many terrible disasters such as happen and will continue to happen as long as human nature remains what it is but which vary in their severity according to the circumstances. For in peace and prosperity States and individuals have milder feelings because people do not then have to face dire necessity; but war which takes away the easy supply of men's daily wants is a harsh schoolmaster and creates in most people correspondingly harsh passions.

And so Greek cities became victims of civil strife and those that fell into this state later, knowing what had been done before carried to still greater extremes the invention of new methods both by the extreme ingenuity of their attacks and the unreasonable extent of their revenges.

The root cause of all these evils was the desire to rule — a desire inspired by greed and ambition — and that fanaticism which is often found in men engaged in political activities. For these who emerged as leaders of political parties in the various city-states each adopted a fair-sounding slogan such as 'political equality for the masses under the law' and the other side would speak of their aim as being 'moderate aristocracy'. Both sides claimed that they aimed only at the well-being of the public; in reality they regarded political power as the prize to be won. Determined to get the better of the other side they undertook the most terrible schemes and aimed at revenges ever more awful pursuing these not within the limit of the law and the public welfare but motivated solely by personal caprice; they would pass an unjust sentence of condemnation or by winning the upper hand through an act of aggression they would satisfy their violent instincts. And a citizen who belonged to neither party was liable to be destroyed by either party for refusing to join their party or perhaps from envy that his neutrality enabled him to survive.

So it came about that every form of evil showed itself in Greece as a result of civil strife in the cities and that straightforward honesty which is the principal element in a noble character was treated with contempt and soon ceased to exist, while the prevailing feeling was one of mutual antipathy and distrust between members of opposing factions.

It was in Corcyra then that most of these atrocities were first committed — all the acts of retaliation and revenge which men who are imbued with fanaticism rather than moderation are likely to commit when their rulers at last give them an opportunity for revenge.

10

The Battle of Mantinea

In battle Greek armies were drawn up facing each other. As far as numbers made it possible each side extended its front line to equal that of the enemy.

A Greek soldier carried a spear or other weapon in his right hand a shield in his left hand. He felt himself to be protected on his left side but vulnerable on the right side. He therefore tended to move to the right to gain some protection from the shield of his comrade on his right. Thus the whole front line on either side edged towards the right creating a danger that the left would be outflanked.

The Battle of Mantinea is interesting because the Lacedaemonian commander, King Agis, to prevent the left of his line from being outflanked ordered some of his troops in the centre to take up a position on the left. But he gave the orders too late and confusion resulted. However the sheer fighting abilities of the Lacedaemonian soldier saved the day for his army.

Thucydides writes:

After this they joined battle, the Argives advancing with haste and fury, the Lacedaemonians slowly and to the music of many flute-players — a custom which has nothing to do with religion but is intended to make the soldiers advance in step with each other, keeping to their ranks and without breaking their order as large armies are apt to do when approaching the enemy line.

Just before the battle began King Agis resolved on the following manoeuvre. All armies are alike in this: on going into action they get extended on their right wing, and one and the other overlap with their adversary's left. The man primarily responsible for this is the first upon the right wing who is always striving to withdraw from the enemy his unarmed side; the same fear makes the rest follow him. On the present occasion the

Mantineans reached with their wing far beyond the Sciritae and the Lacedaemonians and Tegeans still farther beyond the Athenians as their army was the largest. Agis, afraid of his left being surrounded and thinking that the Mantineans outflanked it too far ordered the Sciritae and Brasideans to move out from their place in the ranks and make the line even with the Mantineans and he told the Polemarchs Hipponoidas and Aristocles to fill up the gap thus formed by throwing themselves into it with two companies taken from the right wing, thinking that his right would still be strong enough, and to spare, and that the line fronting the Mantineans would gain in solidity.

However he gave these orders at the moment of attack, at too short notice, and it so happened that Aristocles and Hipponoidas would not move over — for which offence they were afterwards banished from Sparta as having been guilty of cowardice — and the enemy meanwhile closed before the Sciritae (whom Agis, on seeing that the two companies did not move over, ordered to return to their place) had time to fill up the breach in question. However now it was that the Lacedaemonians, completely worsted in respect of skill, showed themselves superior in courage. As soon as they came to close quarters with the enemy, the Mantinean right broke through the Spartan Sciritae and the troops who had been under Brasidas. Then the Mantineans, bursting in with their allies and the thousand picked Argives, into the unclosed breach in their lie, cut up and surrounded the Lacedaemonians and drove them in full flight to the wagons, slaying some of the older men on guard there. But the Lacedaemonians, worsted in this part of the field, with the rest of their army and especially the centre where the three hundred knights, as they are called, fought round King Agis, fell on the older men of the Argives and the five companies so named and on the Cleonaeans, the Orneans and the Athenians next them and at once routed them, the greater number not even waiting to strike a blow but giving way the moment that the enemy came on, some even being trodden under foot in their fear of their assailants.

The army of the Argives and their allies, having given way in this quarter, was now completely cut in two, and the Lacedaemonian and Tegean right simultaneously closing round the Athenians with the troops that outflanked them, these last found themselves placed between two fires, being surrounded on one side and already defeated on the other. Indeed, they would have suffered more severely than any other part of the army but for the services of the cavalry they had with them.

11

Melos

The small island of Melos took no part in the war and wished only to be left alone. But the Athenians, as a maritime power, considered that they had a right to include all islands in their empire. They sent a force to Melos and demanded the submission of the island. Thucydides records the discussion which took place in what is often known, because of the way the speeches are set out as the Melian Dialogue. The argument is conducted on an abstract level, the Athenians asserting that might is right and it is in the best interests of Melos to submit. Typical of the speeches are:

Athenians: *You know as well as we do that right is in question only between equals in power while the strong do what they can and the weak suffer what they must.*

Melians: *How can you avoid making enemies of all existing neutrals who shall look at our case and conclude that one day or another you will attack them?*

This is how Thucydides records the upshot of the matter:

The Athenians now withdrew from the discussion and the Melians, left to themselves came to a decision corresponding to what they had maintained in the discussion and answered, 'Our resolution, Athenians, is the same as it was at first. We will not, in a moment, deprive of freedom a city which has been inhabited seven hundred years.'

The city was besieged and, some treachery taking place inside, the Melian surrendered at discretion to the Athenians, who put to death all the grown men, took and sold all the women and children for slaves and subsequently sent out five hundred colonists and inhabited the place themselves.

THE ATHENIANS IN SICILY

12

The Departure of the Expeditionary Force

*In the middle of their life and death struggle with Sparta the Athenians
formed the insanely ambitious plan of conquering Sicily and so adding
to their own resources the resources of that large and prosperous island.
The expedition strained Athens' resources in men, ships and money and
ended in total defeat for the Athenians. But the expeditionary force left
Athens in high hopes of success.*

Thucydides describes the departure of the expedition.

The expedition departed in mid-summer. Most of the allies, with
the corn transports and smaller craft and the rest of the
expedition, had already received orders to assembly at Corcyra
and from there to cross in a body to the Lapegian promontory.
But the Athenians themselves and any of their allies who
happened to be with them went down to Piraeus upon a day
appointed, at daybreak, and manned the ships for putting out
to sea. With them also went, one might say, the whole population
of the city, both citizens and foreigners. The local people escorted
those that belonged to them, relatives and sons with hope as
they thought of the victories they would win and lamentations
at the prospect that they might never see some of them again,
considering the long voyage they were about to make from their
own country. At this moment when they were about to part from
each other they became more aware of the dangers ahead than
they had been when they voted in favour of the expedition,
although the strength of the armament and the abundant
provision they could see in every department re-assured them.
Foreigners and the rest of the crowd were there to enjoy the
spectacle which was well worth looking at and which passed all

belief. Indeed this armament that first set out was the most splendid and costly that had ever been put together by a single Greek city. (In mere numbers of ships and heavy infantry the expedition against Epidaurus under Pericles (and the force that was sent against Potidaea under Hagnon) was not inferior, containing as it did four thousand Athenian heavy infantry, three hundred horse and one hundred triremes, accompanied by fifty Lesbian and Chian vessels and many allies. But these were sent on a short voyage and with scanty equipment). The present expedition was equipped for a long period of service and for both kinds of fighting, whichever should be required — with ships or with land forces. The fleet had been provided at great expense to the captains and to the State Treasury. The Treasury gave a drachma a day to each seaman and provided empty ships — sixty warships and forty transports manning these with the best crews available. The captains too provided additional pay to the seamen and went to great expense in the equipping and decoration of their vessels, competing with each other in the provision of the finest vessels. The land forces had been chosen from the best muster-rolls and vied with each other in their arms and personal equipment. From this there resulted a rivalry among themselves but an impression among the rest of the Greek world that the whole thing was more a demonstration of power and resources than an expeditionary force against an enemy. For if anyone had added up the public expenditure by the state and the private expenditure of members of the expeditionary force — public expenditure including not only sums already disbursed but the funds entrusted to the commanders and the money spent by individuals on their equipment — and had added the journey money which each combatant was likely to have provided for himself in addition to his pay from the State for such a long voyage and what the soldiers or traders took with them for the purpose of exchange, it would have been found that many talents were being taken out of the country. What made the expeditionary force so memorable was not so much its bold objective and impressive appearance as its overwhelming strength compared with those against whom it was being sent and that this was the longest passage from home hitherto undertaken and the most ambitious in its aims in relation to the resources of the State which undertook it.

The ships being now manned and everything they intended

to take with them having been put on board, a trumpet commanded silence and the customary prayers offered before putting out to sea were offered not in each ship individually but all together following the voice of a herald. Bowls of wine were mixed throughout the whole force and libations in gold and silver goblets were offered by the soldiers and their officers.

13

The Naval Battle in the Great Harbour of Syracuse

The Sicilian campaign went badly for the Athenians. The arrival of reinforcements under the command of Demosthenes (the hero of Pylos) did not turn the scales in favour of the Athenians. It was decided to withdraw the whole expeditionary force. The Athenian fleet was then bottled up in the Great Harbour of Syracuse. The Syracusan navy, which had proved that it was a match for the Athenians, or even superior to them, also lay in the Great Harbour. They had blocked the exits from the harbour to prevent the escape of the Athenians. The Athenian army was extended along the shore of the harbour, well aware that their only hope of returning home lay in the success of their fleet in forcing a way out of the harbour.

Thucydides describes the battle and the emotions of those present:

The Syracusan generals and Gylippus had just concluded their addresses to their men when they saw that the Athenians were manning their vessels. So they gave orders to man their ships.

Meanwhile Nicias (the Athenian commander) distraught by the situation in which he was placed and seeing how great was the danger facing the Athenians and how near, for their ships were about to push off from the shore, thought, as men are wont to think in such a crisis, that there was something more that ought to be done and something more that ought to be said. So he called the captains of the ships to him and addressing each by his father's name as well as by his own name and by his tribe adjured each not to belie his good name and reputation and the virtues of his ancestors for which they were famous. He reminded them that they came from a city which was the free-est of the free where everyone enjoyed an unfettered discretion to live as he pleased and added other arguments such as one would use at time of crisis and which, with but few alterations, are made to serve on all such occasions — appeals to wives, children and national gods without caring whether these appeals might be regarded as commonplace clichés but loudly invoking them in the belief that they would be effective in the present crisis. Having thus admonished his captains not as he would but as best he could, Nicias led the army down to the edge of the harbour and extended the troops as widely as possible so as to give encouragement to the men in the ships. Demosthenes, Menander and Eurydemus who took command on board the ships, put out from their own camp and sailed straight for the barricade and to the passage left open for an exit intending to force their way out. The Syracusans and their allies had already put out with about the same number of ships as before. Part of their fleet was on guard and at the outlet from the harbour while the rest were placed all round the harbour so that they could fall upon the Athenians from every direction while the army was placed round the edge of the harbour to give help wherever it was required. The Syracusan fleet was commanded by Siracus and Agatharchus who each had a wing of the whole fleet while Pythen and the Corinthians were in the centre.

When the rest of the Athenians came up to the barrier they overpowered the ships stationed there by the force of their initial charge, and began to loosen the fastenings. From there the fighting spread to the whole harbour with the Syracusans and their allies taking part vigorously. The fighting was more intense than it had ever been before. On either side the crews showed great zeal in bringing up their ships at the boatswain's orders. The helmsmen showed consummate skill in manoeuvring and in efforts to outdo each other. When ships came to grips with each other the soldiers on board did their best not to let the part they played be inferior to that played by the others. Each man endeavoured to show himself outstanding.

Many ships were engaged in a small area (for these were the largest fleets fighting in the narrowest space ever known, the combined fleets numbering little less than two thousand ships). Consequently there were not many attacks made by ramming amidships for there was not sufficient space to backwater after the ramming or space to break away. Collisions caused by one ship happening to run foul of another when one was trying to escape or was about to attack were very frequent. All the time when a vessel was coming up to attack another vessel the men on deck hurled javelins, arrows and stones on the enemy ship but once the two vessels were alongside each other the heavy infantry on each vessel tried to board the other vessel. Because of the narrowness of the space it often happened that a vessel was charging an enemy vessel on one side while being charged by another enemy ship on the other side so that the helmsman had to consider the need to attack and to evade being attacked; the helmsman having to consider not just one thing at a time but two separate things. The great din caused by ships crashing into each other increased the terror and made it almost impossible to hear orders shouted by helmsmen. In the excitement there was much shouting of encouragement by boatswains — to the Athenians urging them to breech the barrier and now if ever to exert themselves to the utmost to get to the safety of their native land. The boatswains on the other side shouted to their men that it would be a splendid thing to prevent the escape of the enemy fleet and so to win glory for their mother countries.

As for the two armies on the shore, so long as the issue of the sea battle was in the balance they were in an agony of conflicting emotions, the Syracusans longing for even greater glory than they had already won, the invaders fearful that they might soon be in even worse circumstances than they were now. For the Athenians everything depended on their navy. Their fears for the future were such as they had never before experienced and as the battle swung this way and that so inevitably did their feelings as they watched from the land. Close to the scene of action and not all looking at the same part of the action, some saw their friends victorious and were enheartened and cheered loudly and called upon the gods not to rob them of their chance of safety, while others, seeing an incident where their own side was worsted, gave vent to cries of alarm or groans of despair. Others again were gazing on some spot where the battle was evenly contested. As their hopes and fears swung this way and that so did their bodies swing from side to side. These were in the worst situation and they suffered more, probably, than the contestants themselves, for all the time they were on the verge of victory or on the point of destruction. In short, in that one Athenian army as long as the issue was in dispute you could hear every kind of sound, groans of despair,

78

shouts of joy, cries of 'we are winning' or 'we are losing' and other cries such as you might expect from a large army afraid and in great peril.

At last after the battle had lasted a long time the Syracusans and their allies broke the Athenian resistance and with much shouting and cheering drove them to the shore. All the crews except those that had been captured when their ships were afloat now got ashore, some this way and others that way and all rushed towards their camp. The land army, no longer swayed by changing emotions but moved by a common impulse, ran, some going down to the ships to help them, others to defend what remained of their wall and others — already the greater part of them — thought only of how to save themselves. The panic was greater than any they had ever experienced. They now suffered themselves very nearly what they had inflicted on the Lacedaemonians at Pylos. As then the Lacedaemonians with the loss of their fleet lost the possibility of recovering the men who had crossed to the island, so now the Athenians had no hope of getting away safely by land unless some miracle occurred.

The sea-fight having been very severe and many ships and men having been lost on both sides the victorious Syracusans and their allies picked up their wrecks and their dead and sailed back to the city where they set up a trophy. But the Athenians overwhelmed by their misfortune never even asked permission to pick up their dead but wanted to retreat that very night. Demosthenes, however, went to Nicias and gave it as his opinion that they should man the ships and make another attempt the next morning to force their way through the exit. He said that they still had more serviceable ships than the enemy; they had sixty and the enemy less than fifty. Nicias agreed with him and was willing to put to sea but the sailors refused to go aboard not believing in the possibility of their success, so overwhelmed were they by their defeat.

14

*The Athenian Expeditionary force after the defeat in the
Great Harbour*

*After their defeat in the sea battle in the Great Harbour the Athenians
decided to withdraw from Syracuse by land. Thucydides describes the scene
on their departure.*

The departure of the army took place on the second day after
the fight in the harbour. It was a lamentable scene, not merely
because they were retreating, their fleet destroyed, their high
hopes dashed and they themselves and the State in peril, but
also, in leaving the camp there were scenes very grievous to
contemplate. The dead lay unburied, and as each man
recognized a friend among them he shuddered with guilt and
horror, while the living who were to be left behind because they
were wounded or sick were far more to be pitied than the dead.
They entreated the living soldiers with many tears to let them
accompany the army until the departing soldiers did not know
what to do when the sick and wounded clung to them begging
to be taken with the army and their comrades. They followed
the army until their strength failed them and then they cried
aloud to heaven until, still shrieking, they were left behind. Filled
with tears and distracted by these terrible scenes, the army found
it hard to go even though they were leaving a hostile country
where they had suffered much. Depression and self-
condemnation were rife among them. They could only be
compared to people escaping from a starved-out town — and
that not a small one for the whole army on the march was not
less than forty thousand men. All carried anything they could
that might be of use. The heavily armed troops and the

80

horsemen, contrary to custom carrying their own rations and supplies, some from lack of servants, others from distrust of them; these had for some time past been deserting and were now doing so in greater numbers. Yet even so they did not carry enough for there was little food left in the camp. Moreover the disgrace and the universality of their sufferings though mitigated to some extent by being widely shared were still felt at the present moment to be a heavy burden especially when they compared the splendour and glory of their departure with their present condition.

For this was the greatest reversal that ever befell a fallen army. They had come intending to enslave others and were departing in fear of being enslaved themselves. They had set out on the expedition with prayers and paeans and now they were preparing to return with all the omens against them. They were proceeding on foot rather than aboard ships, trusting not in their fleet but in their heavy infantry.

Nicias seeing the army dejected and very different from what it had once been, moved along the ranks speaking words of encouragement and comfort. As he went along he raised his voice to a louder and louder pitch as though determined that his words should reach as many as possible. He addressed them in this way.

'Athenians and allies, even in our present circumstances there are grounds for hope. Before now men have been saved from worse situations than this. And you must not condemn yourselves too severely for the recent disasters or for your present undeserved sufferings. Look at yourselves. Mark how many and how efficient are the heavy infantry marching in your ranks. Do not be too despondent. Reflect on the fact that you yourselves are a city wherever you establish yourselves and there is no other city in Sicily which could easily resist your attack, or expel you when once you are firmly established. As to the march you yourselves must see to its good order and that it is safely conducted. And let this thought be in the mind of every man, that on whatever spot he is forced to fight that spot he must conquer and hold as his homeland and stronghold. Meanwhile we must push on by day and by night for the provisions we carry with us are scanty. If we can reach some friendly place of the Sicels who from fear of the Syracusans are still loyal to us, then you may forthwith consider yourselves safe. Word has been sent to them to meet us with supplies of food.

'To sum up, be convinced, soldiers, that you must be brave for there is no place here where cowardice can find a safe shelter. If you now escape the enemy you may obtain what your hearts desire. You who are Athenians will raise up the great power of the city, fallen so low as it is now. For it is men that make a city, not walls or empty ships.'

Thus Nicias encouraged the troops. Moving up and down the column, if he saw any stragglers or men not in the right ranks he took them to their places and set them there. Meanwhile Demosthenes did the same for his part of the army speaking to them in a similar way.

The Syracusans put any Athenians and their allies whom they captured in the stone quarries, for this seemed the safest place to hold them.

The prisoners in the quarries were at first hardly treated by the Syracusans. They were crowded together in a narrow hole without a roof to cover them. A large number of them confined in a small space, they were tormented by the heat of the sun and the stifling atmosphere and the nights which were autumnal and chilly made them ill through the sudden change in temperature. Besides as they had to do everything in the same place because of want of room and the bodies of those who died from their wounds, or from the violent change in temperature, or from other causes were left heaped together one on top of another, an intolerable stench arose. Hunger and thirst never ceased to afflict them, each man during eight months having only half a pint of water and a pint of corn given him daily. In short no single kind of suffering to be experienced by men thrust into such a place was spared them. For some seventy days they thus lived all together; after which, all except the Athenians and any Siceliots or Italiots who had joined in the expedition were sold. The total number of prisoners taken it would be difficult to state exactly, but it could not have been less than seven thousand.

This was the greatest Hellenic action in the war and in my opinion in Hellenic history. For the victors it was most glorious and to the defeated the most calamitous. For they were beaten at all points and in every way. They were destroyed as the saying is with a total destruction — their fleet, their army — everything was destroyed and few out of many returned home.

15

Athens: The Aftermath of the Sicilian Disaster

When news of the Sicilian disaster reached Athens, for a long time nobody believed even the most trustworthy of the soldiers who had escaped and returned home. A disaster so complete was considered incredible. When the conviction was at last forced upon them, they were angry with the orators who had spoken in the Assembly in favour of the expedition — forgetting that they themselves had voted in favour of the expedition. They were angry too with the recitals of oracles and soothsayers and those concerned with omens who had encouraged them to believe that they could conquer Sicily.

The State was already under pressure from many quarters and this latest disaster caused alarm and the greatest consternation. The deaths of so many soldiers and sailors caused private grief to their families and friends and the State itself felt the loss of so large a part of its manpower and of its fleet. When people realized that they had not enough men to replace their losses, not enough ships to make up for those destroyed and not enough money in the Treasury to pay for replacements, they began to despair of the future. They thought that their enemies in Sicily would immediately sail against Piraeus, buoyed up by confidence after their recent success and their enemies at home would now redouble their efforts to attack them by land and sea and their allies would revolt. Nevertheless it was determined that with such resources as they had, they would resist to the end, obtaining timber from wherever they could, and money, and they resolved to equip a fleet as fast as they could and to take action to secure their allies, especially Euboea, and to introduce economic reforms in the city and for that purpose to appoint a commission of older citizens who should advise on the state of affairs as occasion should arise. In short, as is the way of democracies when they were terrified they were prepared to take prudent measures.

In the following winter all Hellas, stirred by the Sicilian disaster, turned against Athens. Neutrals thought that even if uninvited they should move against Athens. They reflected that Athens would probably have attacked each of them had the Sicilian campaign been successful. The war would soon be over and it would be to their advantage if they had taken part in it. The allies of the Lacedaemonians were more eager than ever to put an end to their weary labour. But above all the States subject to Athens showed a readiness to revolt, beyond their ability and resources, judging the present situation in a fanatical manner and refusing to listen to any suggestion that Athens might be able to last out the coming summer.

Beyond all this, the Lacedaemonians were encouraged by the prospect of being joined in the spring by their Sicilian allies with the fleet which necessity had compelled them to acquire. With so many reasons for confidence the Lacedaemonians resolved to throw themselves into the war without reserve. Considering that once it was successfully concluded they would be rid of the danger which would have confronted them if Athens had been able to add the resources of Sicily to her own and they themselves would establish a secure hegemony over the whole of Greece.

Their King, Agis, accordingly set out that winter with some troops from Decelea, levied from the allies contributions for the fleet, and made other preparation for recommencing hostilities in the spring.

In the meantime the Athenians went ahead with the measures they had agreed on. They collected timber for shipbuilding, fortified Cape Sunium to make it safer for grain-bearing ships to round the promontory, abandoned the fort they had built in Laconia while they also for economy cut down any other expenditure that seemed unnecessary. Above all they kept a close watch on their allies to prevent any defection.